Unbroken

By

Lakia McDaniel

Unbroken

Copyright © by Lakia McDaniel

All rights reserved 2014

NEW BREED PUBLISHING

ISBN 13: 978-0-9833438-3-7

ISBN 10: 0983343837

Library of Congress Cat. Num. in-pub.-Data

PRINTED IN THE UNITED STATES OF AMERICA

New Breed Publishing presents:

Unbroken; A story of struggle, faith, and triumph

This book is a work of non-fiction. The author intentionally left names of individuals out to protect their privacy and maintain their anonymity. Throughout this book are periods of shared personal events and experiences of the author, followed with the unsolicited advice from a personal standpoint. No part of this book is written with advice from a professional counselor or therapist.

Cover Image by: Jarvis Hall of Starks Enterprises

Design by: Kreative Solutions by Mahogani/Tanisha Pettiford

Editing/Typesetting; Illuminnessence Publishing/Allison Edwards

Dedicated to those who have difficulty finding their happy place.

Introduction

If you would have asked me three years ago if I know what peace feels like, I wouldn't have known. Now, I can honestly say that I have found peace and I feel it every day. It starts with the moment I open my eyes during the morning's sunrise, and ends with my nightly conversation with God as the moon kisses the sky amidst the stars.

I used to struggle with self to the point of being lost within my own soul. My needless suffering was due to lack of knowledge of who I really am. I was confused and wasn't totally clear about the path and direction I wanted to take in my life. My struggles with men were apparent. I've dealt with a few heartaches too many, in retrospect were caused by my own accord. I've attributed to the unsuccessful connections with the men in my past.

Of course, I didn't realize that back then. I take full responsibility of how things went down with them. I explain how later in the book. My financial struggles hindered my confidence as a responsible adult. My poor monetary choices included bad investments and loans which I am currently trying to pay back. As a result, I now have to be careful with how I spend money. I'm going through all of that, as I continue to deal with the loss of one of my children. That will also be addressed and how I'm in the process of overcoming it.

In this book, you'll read page by page the true testimony of my life. I'll share where I've been, and where I currently am emotionally, spiritually, and financially. I may have gone through situations that could have broken my spirit, my happiness, my confidence, and my love for self. As you read the pages, you'll come to understand that I am and will always be...unbroken.

Chapter 1

"Girls are afraid of being alone. Women revel in it, using the time for personal growth." ~Unknown

I thought I had it all together while in my twenties. Looking back, I was clearly messed up in the head and in the heart. Although I've had jobs, my own place, a car, and no kids to limit my opportunities, I still felt stuck in a place that hindered my internal growth. I was single and didn't like it. I dated on occasion, but didn't connect well with men. When I say "didn't connect", that doesn't mean I didn't know how to talk to men. It means I was somewhat delusional in their intentions of me to the point where I thought they were into me when in fact, they weren't. From the time I've graduated high school, I wanted to be in love and in a relationship badly. I wanted to experience what it felt like to be in a loving presence of a man. I wanted to have what the couples had in dramatic movies and romance novels. I wanted to relate to what the R&B singer was singing about on the radio. I knew all of the aforementioned was obviously glamorized and glorified for entertainment purposes, but it was what I wanted to feel in my reality.

I wanted to feel cared for and loved, and I often wondered why it was such a tedious job for me to find the "perfect" guy. The few that I was involved with all had potential to be "the one", until they showed their ass. It's been the same with most of the guys I had encountered. We'd meet, have phone conversations, get to know each other more by going on a few dates, have sex, have more phone conversations, have more sex, etc. As the weeks went by the dates became fewer and the calls became limited, until we'd stop talking altogether. I'm left wondering what happened and what went wrong that we stopped connecting. I felt used and confused after every guy I became involved with. That particular issue with men lasted all the way up into my mid thirties, including my children's father with whom the relationship lasted nine years.

I met my children's father in the year of 2000. We became romantically involved in 2001, had our first child in 2003, became engaged and moved in together in 2005. We had our second child in 2006, and our third child in 2007. We broke up in 2009, but in between the bearing of children and trying to play "wifey", I lost sense of self. Although we've never made it to the altar, I've provided as a wife, because that was what HE wanted and I loved him...so I thought.

My goals were put to the side, because I was too busy with being a Mommy and trying to make him happy. I was angry at him, because I felt he didn't acknowledge that. That issue, as well as other issues eventually led to our break up. We've both came to the realization that we were better off co-parenting. Today, we are cordial, and friendly towards one another. We still have our disagreements, but we're at a much better place now than when we were together.

The lesson that I've learned from that relationship was that I was in love with being in love. After I moved in with him, it became apparent to me that loving the person he is was a struggle. His intentions for our relationship and how I SHOULD be was diminishing my light when I wanted both our lights to shine together. As a result, I did what I had to do, which was pack my things and my kids' things and move out. Since then, I started my journey to find Lakia. I needed to seek the fire that would help get my light shining the way it's supposed to, and let me tell you...it wasn't easy.

I moved in with my cousin who was gracious enough to take me in, even with her two teenage kids. It wasn't my own place, but it would be my home for the next year. I didn't mind living with her, and I was absolutely grateful for a place to stay for myself and my children. Moving out had provided a release of bad weight, and I felt so good to get out from where I was. I had gained better insight on why things turned out the way they had.

I accepted what happened and used it for motivation to get back on my feet career wise. I moved in with my cousin with the mindset that living on my own was my ultimate goal, but in the back of my mind, my not so good credit prevented me from taking that extra leap into finding resources for first time home ownership and as a result, I got comfortable.

During that time I was finally able to use my time to focus on my goal as an author. Moving out also gave me the freedom to date again. My writing career was finally taking off, as I had published my first novel *Hidden Confessions*, but my dating life was going nowhere. Of course, I didn't see it then, because I thought I had something special with this guy I became involved with. After weeks of phone calls, texts, and Facebooking, we had finally decided to go on our first date.

Our first date eventually became our only date, but he was still calling and texting me every day, so I let him get away with that because I liked him. He remained consistent with everything except going out together. Consistency is very important to me, so I gave him the benefit of the doubt, especially since he's a single father. The downside to our relationship was the constant negativity about his ex-wife. We could not have a conversation without her name being brought up. It frustrated me to no end but I didn't say anything, because I didn't want to appear insincere about his problems with her. It was my opportunity to show him who the better woman was for him.

According to what he told me, she wasn't shit. The more badly he talked about her, the more it made me feel better about our relationship. Forget the fact that he only took me out once out of the year we've been involved. Forget the fact that our nights together only included a movie on cable and sex which followed afterwards. I made sure it was the best sex I could give him. I made sure it was a movie he really would be interested in seeing!

Overall, I worked on becoming the woman HE would want. His kids would adore me. His mother would adore me, too! I was going to be his...until I realized one night that he was still in love with his ex-wife. He didn't have to say it. It was all in the tears he shed about her, after having sex with me. At that moment, the little confidence I had for myself started to deteriorate.

There was nothing I could do or say to help this man recover from what was going on in his life. My energy was depleted from trying to keep this man focused on us. Needless to say, I stopped dealing with him intimately. From then, I regained my energy through constant prayer and talks with God. I spent more time with my kids, and I worked. The recent release of my novel afforded me more free time to focus on my career and family.

My kids are everything to me and every single day I prove how much of a great mother I am, even when there's no one to prove it to. That has a lot to do with the guilt of being in front of a computer daily. With my career as an author and running an online magazine, I feel bad that I have to do spend time online, as much as spending quality time with the kids. I try to balance it all out, because I know that creating memories with my children is a priority in my life.

I also want to become a success with everything that I do, because I want my children to look at me some day and say "That's MY mommy!" As mothers, we naturally want to take the sickness away when our children become ill or take the pain away when they become hurt. So, I'm sure parents or even folks that aren't parents can understand that it was undoubtedly the worst day of my life when my youngest son passed from a sudden illness.

Chapter 2

"Motherhood is near to divinity. It is the highest, holiest service to be assumed by mankind." ~ Howard   W.   Hunter

I love my kids so much. Before I had any, I couldn't see myself with them. I wanted to live selfishly by spending freely without the confines to saving for pampers and milk. I wanted to come and go as I please, and not have to worry about a sitter. My cousins and friends all had kids at a young age, so I saw what they went through as struggling single mothers. I wasn't ready for any of that.

Now that I have my children, I can't see myself without them. Although one of them is not here physically, I still manage to move on and care for my other two children. It's something that I'm shocked about sometimes. As a mother, you'll never want to have to bury your child, but I had to do it. I've had weak moments since the death of my baby boy, but my strength definitely outweighs the weak moments. I never knew I had that much strength in me, until becoming and staying strong was my only option.

I have one girl and two boys, and it's amazing to me that the way they came into this world is how you'd describe what kind of person they are. For instance, my oldest child Shenya took fifteen hours to make her grand entrance. To this day, she is as slow as a turtle. It takes her a little longer for her to get ready for school.

My second child Kenneth was in so much of a hurry that by the time I arrived at the hospital to have him, I was fully dilated and ready to push. He wouldn't even give me time to get epidural administered! To this day, he is considered my boy who likes to rush through life's little treasures, instead of taking the time to learn and manifest. For instance, he skips a few holes of his buttoned down shirts, and still doesn't notice before walking out the house.

My third child Robert gave me a few hours before entering the world. Even pushing him out was the most pleasant out of the three. Robert in his short years was very easy-going and pretty neutral with time. I'll never know if he would have outgrown that. Overall, my kids are my gifts. They are really my only blessings out of that nine year relationship. Something I can actually thank their father for.

As a receiver of precious gifts, you try your best to keep them protected from harm. That's why as parents, we feel bad when our children fall and bruise their knee, or become sick. We want to take the pain away, because we don't like to see them cry. That's why when I learned that my youngest child died and how, I felt that I failed as a protector and as a mother.

It was on a Tuesday when I dropped them off at their dads for a few days. Robert appeared fine and healthy as an ox. He didn't as so much coughed or sneezed, so when his dad informed me the next day that he wasn't feeling well and felt hot, I was a bit surprised. I didn't think much of it, considering that my children have developed fevers before, so I did what I thought any mother would do. I bought some medication to lower his fever and expected him to get better after that.

I stopped by his dad's to check on my babies before work the next morning. There Robert was, lying on the sofa with the most somber look in his eyes. It almost made me cry. When you look at Robert, his face was usually bright, with big bright eyes, and a smile that would melt your heart. I immediately gave him medication to lower his fever and stayed with him, until it was time for me to go work. Their dad was still in the middle of his fatherly duties, so I reminded him to keep him hydrated and to call me if he doesn't get any better. Thursday, their dad called me to inform me that he felt better enough to get up and play with his siblings. When I heard that, I assumed I had nothing to worry about. I breathed a sigh of relief, thinking my baby pulled through, and I didn't have to make a trip to the

ER. The next day, Friday, I decided to get my children since their dad had them for the past few days. My plans were to take them home and spend the ultimate quality time with them. We were going to get some snacks, and watch all of their favorite cartoons. We were going to go to the playground, and do other things that make them happy. All of those plans were crushed when things changed unexpectedly.

I stopped by their school to pick up the kids early, because I wanted to take advantage of the beautiful day. The sun was beaming in the midst of the 50 degree day, which was unusually warm for it to be January. I get there only to find out that their dad had already picked them up. I figured he made similar plans. I drive to his house, which was a short distance from the school. When I arrived and parked in front of his door, I was so eager to see my children, particularly Robert considering his past few days were a bit rough for him. I anticipated my weekend with them as I rang the door bell. It was my day off and the slight smile on my face expressed how good I was feeling. I didn't expect to see what I saw when their dad opened the front door. He frantically opened the front door with Robert's half naked body cradled in his arms.

"He's not breathing!" Their dad yelled, as I ran in behind him, screaming.

He laid him down on the sofa, and I dressed him as quickly as I could, while his siblings looked on. It was apparent that their dad was trying to dress him, since he was still undressed from the waist down with only underwear and socks. The only thing I chose to do was put on his jacket and a pair of jeans.

Although, the ambulance was already called, I picked up my baby boy instead and ran out of the house with him. I carefully placed him in his car seat, and jumped into the front seat. A couple of neighbors looked on with concern, as I pulled off with urgency. As I drove with much acceleration as I possibly could on a city street, I prayed one thousand prayers that my son would pull through. With every stop light that I drove pass, I screamed at the top of my lungs, asking why?

When I arrived at the hospital, I immediately parked at the most convenient parking spot, not caring if I was to get towed. All I had on my mind was that Robert would survive. I still prayed as I picked up my baby boy and ran towards the front of the hospital. There, outside was a male nurse taking a smoke break. He saw me in such a dire need, that he immediately dropped his cigarette and ran towards me. I allowed him to take Robert from my arms, and he ran inside the emergency room to the nearest bed. Of course, I followed him, as I pleaded frantically with everyone to save my baby. There were onlookers, including the staff who were there within eye shot and those who were waiting to be seen by doctors but I didn't care. All I cared about was my baby breathing again.

They began working on Robert, as they walked me into another room. I reluctantly walked away, and as I looked back at him, I saw the work of CPR being administered to his lifeless body.

To this day, I don't know the woman who talked with me and prayed with me that everything would be okay but I couldn't believe her. As each minute passed and as every second ticked on the clock conveniently placed in the waiting room, all I could do was remember the short life of the little boy who I loved dearly and spent three years with. The precious moments replayed in my head as if in a movie of times when he and his siblings made me laugh. Those moments could never be forgotten or replaced.

All I could think of was that he has so much living to do. I thought that God wouldn't break my heart like this. NOT LIKE THIS. I needed to see him grow up into the handsome, respectful, and productive adult that he was supposed to be. He was supposed to watch cartoons with me and his siblings right now so he can't die. Not after what I promised I would do for him and his siblings this weekend. Not after what I promised to do for him for the rest of his life.

I promised him that I would take care of him, but I failed. During that moment, I felt like I've truly failed as a mother. I was in my opinion a failure, because my son was in another room fighting for his life. He is too young to fight. As his mother, I am to fight for him, always.

After what seemed like an eternity, a black middle-aged doctor walked in to give an update. From the look on his eyes as he sat next to me, the news was not going to be good. In my heart, I wanted my son to breathe again, but I sensed the reality of it as I watched this man. I waited for an answer that I knew would change my life forever. His reluctance in telling me the news was reflective on his face. I could tell it was nothing but sad news. I still asked hoping for the best, as I pleaded with him to tell me that my son made it. He couldn't even verbally respond and did so by shaking his head no. My world crumbled right then and there. I fell to my knees and screamed at the top of my lungs "My baby! My baby!"

I kept asking God why, as I felt like he punished me for whatever wrong I've done in my life. Never in a million years would I expect any of my children to die. It's something you'd never imagine as a parent, because one of your goals in life is for them to bury you. All I kept thinking from that moment on was that Robert didn't deserve this. He didn't deserve to depart this earth so soon.

After about 30 minutes to gather my composure, the nurse allowed me to go into Robert's room to say my goodbyes. The room was different from the one they originally placed him in. When I walked in, the room was at an appropriately dark setting. Robert's body was dressed in a hospital gown, and I could tell he was placed in his bed with care. His covers were tucked perfectly over him with the top part of it folded at his waistline with precision.

His head was turned to his right, which was perfect for me to lie next to him and give him a million kisses. I talked with Robert about the cartoons we were supposed to watch, and how much I wanted him to open his eyes. I lifted his covers to look at his body one last time, and I remember how stiff he was and how surprisingly elongated his body looked. I never saw a dead body so up close and unfortunately, I had to experience it for the first time with my own child.

Between crying my eyes out, I just stared at him. I played with his eyelids, rubbed his head, and parted his lips to check his teeth. During this time, I continued to shed more tears until my eyes couldn't form any more. The autopsy revealed that Robert died from a severe respiratory infection. Some say that they observe me and wonder how I remain so strong since my son's passing. I tell them all the time that it's only by the grace of God that I'm able to pull through and move on with life.

At first, I thought God was punishing me, but I prayed and talked with him until I've realized that children are our gifts, but they are not ours. They are HIS. They are GOD's children. It's our job to raise them to be respectful and productive citizens of this world that God has created. Our children are only meant to be here for a certain length of time. When God sees fit to have his angels, he will send them up. For he knows how strong we can be, so he'll never put us through anything we cannot handle.

I thought I would never get over my son leaving us, until I've realized that I had no other option, but to "be". I still have two other kids to raise and be strong for. Within that personal understanding along with spiritual guidance, and my huge support system, I am the strong person that you see today. Robert's death took everything in me NOT to blame myself for what happened. Both his father and I did what any parent would do. Robert was just meant to be here for only a few short years. He was too precious to be consumed with life within an earthly world, and I've accepted that.

With such life obstacles, I'm just blessed to be able to go on with life with a sane mind. Life can definitely be arduous, but what doesn't kill you will make you stronger. I know of and heard of other parents that lost children. Some died in such a horrendous or violent manner, and some parents lost more than one. I look at them and wonder how they can go on and that actually motivates me more, because it means

I'm not alone. They've also proven to me that you can overcome.

For me, it's not only about overcoming death, but overcoming life, as well. Dealing with death is one thing, but dealing with the daily challenges of life can be overwhelming. Overall, I've struggled with motherhood, death, men, money, and love of self. All of those could have eventually led me to a pit of self-destruction, but I didn't let that happen.

The whole purpose for writing this book is to show you how I overcame all of those and didn't let any of what happened destroy me. It wasn't easy and to be honest, I still have those days when I'll just say "fuck it all" but instead, I put on my big girl panties and I keep it moving. I did it not just for myself, but for my kids so they can see what not giving up in life looks like. Robert's death has taught me to enjoy life more. Learn life, live life, breathe life, see life, eat life, drink life, and embrace life as it is. Life is what we make it, so it's up to us to make the proper choices that will help nourish us as productive, loving beings. All of that includes learning from our failures in order to become a success in whatever we choose to be or do. I have taken the past few years to learn the importance of self love. By loving myself, I have learned to accept no less than what I deserve in life.

Loving me will also show the universe what I deserve and in return, the universe gives me what I deserve. It's called the law of attraction. If I want love, I'll have to love myself first. If I want consistency, I'll have to work on staying consistent with myself. If I want success, I'll have to stay committed and focused, and I will be blessed with it. All of what I ask for was never hard to gain. I just had to check myself in order to get it.

Chapter 3

"There are people who have money and people who are rich"~ Coco Chanel

M y quest to become "rich" has been a mission of mine ever since my first full time job as a dental assistant. I consider myself a hard worker, but unfortunately it hasn't paid off due to extreme irresponsibility with money. Even when I didn't have many bills and no children, I had invested a lot of my money in clothes, trips to the hair salon every two weeks, and bad investments with "get rich quick" schemes that I was gullible enough to trust. I was in my twenties, living in my own apartment right underneath my mother in the same building. I didn't see that I was wasting money, because I thought I was being responsible. As long as my rent was paid, as well as other bills such as my car insurance, cable, and phone bill you couldn't tell me that I wasn't handling business.

If I only knew to keep money in my bank account and prepare for the future, I'd be a lot better off. Instead, my bank account stayed in the negative, and whatever I had left from paying my bills I spent on unnecessary stuff. I was never taught the value of saving a buck, micromanaging, and the importance of growing your dollars. I've managed money like this going into my thirties. Even after I had my kids, I still did not take in the importance of building my funds. I became really comfortable with living pay check to pay check. That is, until I had enough of doing so. It took a car re-possession, losing a house, and getting terminated from one of my many dental assisting jobs for me to become more responsible with money. Not only that, I had my publishing business that needed to flourish.

I want to say that having money affects my mood. If I don't have enough of it, I become depressed, constantly thinking I can't do this or get that. These thoughts consumed me a great deal most of my adult life, especially since I've started my publishing company. Money is a powerful piece of paper to be able to alter someone's mood. Without it, we'll feel useless and become disabled from achieving many things, dreams, goals, and passions. That didn't stop me from owning a couple of credit cards that I had eventually maxed out. Of course, I had intended to pay them back but didn't expect setbacks like losing my jobs. I had to resort to making decisions between paying my car insurance and going without my cable for a month or two. Either way, that credit card bill had to wait, hence the debt I had accumulated.

Being eligible for government assistance like food stamps definitely helped with keeping a little money in my pockets, as well as keeping a stocked fridge. To this day, it seems like the taller my children get, the greedier they become. Today, with growing children, a business to support, and a house I'm trying to purchase, I've recently had an epiphany. It finally dawned on me that I have all of these opportunities in front of me to become successful financially, as well as become more emotionally stable. Most importantly, I had the opportunity to build a closer relationship with God. Instead, I hadn't been doing anything with the opportunities bestowed upon me.

As a result of my epiphany, I had decided to finally make the changes I needed to make within myself. I had to believe in my dreams, rid the fear of failure that I was carrying, and take action. I'll bet you're wondering...if I had problems with mismanaging money, how was I able to start a publishing company?

When you are determined and persistent about something, you'll make it happen. I was determined to publish my own book, so I put enough money together to start it. I've come to the realization that if I can be persistent with putting my dream as a publisher into fruition, then I shouldn't have a problem being persistent with everything else in my life. The key factor that kept me from evolving was my inability to stay focused, see my self-worth, and suffering from the fear of failure in all aspects of my life. My life felt stagnant and every time I took three steps forward, it felt as if I was pushed five steps back.

In the next few chapters, I will show how I have improved in the areas of self love, motherhood, dealing with men, and financial status. Within these pages, I hope that you all will find the motivation and courage to change what's challenging in your life. By you reading this book, you have already proved that you're committed to that, as well as finding little old me interesting...and for that I appreciate you. For some time, I struggled with when I should release this book, because I felt like my story wasn't finished. To this day, I still feel like I'm living my story chapter by chapter.

Honestly, I believe I am until God calls me to the heavens. When I decided to finally transition my story into written words, I felt an obligation to share with those who could be looking for answers, validation, or reassurance in living a happier life beyond life's challenges, including death of a loved one. Also, there's no perfect time to share my story like the present, because my story is about never-ending progression.

It's about trying times, love lost, love gained, losing self, finding self, losing hope, finding hope, struggle, empowerment, proud moments, sad moments, real moments, disappointments, forgiveness, acceptance, lessons, intimacy, success, responsibility, actions, persistence, feeling anew, being ME, being YOU, being US....becoming unbroken.

Chapter 4

"When a woman becomes her own best friend life is easier"~ *Diane Von Furstenberg*

With the help of books like *"Women Who Love Too Much"* by Robin Norwood, as well as my many life lessons, I've discovered that it was me who was the common denominator in the relationships I've had with the men in my life. Looking back, I see the many mistakes I have caused. I've realized that what I gave wasn't asked for. I've assumed instead of utilizing my voice for communication, and the biggest mistake was that I didn't understand, even though I am a good woman, I'll never be good enough for a man who isn't ready for a committed relationship.

One day, I picked up a pen and pad and compiled a list of guidelines for myself that I've implemented into my life. It was then when I realized the only way I could prevent becoming hurt in half-ass relationships was to evolve from feeling like only a man's love and attention validates my fierceness, or that being with a man makes me feel whole. I had to believe that I'm already fierce and beautiful, and if a man doesn't see neither, it's simply isn't for him to see and I'll be okay with that.

I want to share my guidelines with you in hopes that you could benefit from it, so here it goes...

- **When you meet someone, be honest of your intentions from the beginning.** Whether you are dating for the purpose to find "the one", or to simply get to know the person, let him know. Ask him what his intentions are, as well. There's nothing worse than dating someone and you're uncertain of his intentions for you. Find out ASAP. It'll save you from a lot of wondering, assuming, and possible disappointment.

- **When a man tells you he's not ready, believe him**

  Not even great sex will make a man change his mind about entering a committed relationship with you. Unless he verbally expresses that he loves you and only wants to be with you, he is free to date others. Don't get mad at him for keeping it 100 from the get-go.

- **Stop doing "wifey" things for boyfriends**

  A lot of times, we do so much for our boyfriends, thinking it will be reciprocated. This is nothing but emotional manipulation. Nine times out of ten, he didn't ask for the one hour massage, the Xbox 360 for his birthday gift, or dinner at an expensive restaurant that YOU chose to pay for. All of the aforementioned is to prove that you're a good woman. If he truly knows you, he would already know you're a good woman. You shouldn't have to do "wifey" things for a guy who you aren't even engaged to in order to validate that fact.

- **A man who shows consistency is a man who is really interested in you.**

When a man is really into you, he will show it with calls, texts, and any other forms of communication. A man will also do anything in his power to spend time with you. If it feels like you have to fight for quality time, then he really isn't that into you. Move on.

- **He will not commit to you, because you're helping him get over an ex.**

  This is pretty much self-explanatory. If anything, you're definitely rebound booty.

- **Put yourself first. Love yourself first. You are worthy of the love you desire**

  Love yourself tremendously, because you know that's how much love you want. When you meet someone, they will see that and try to match the abundance of love that you give yourself. Treat your mind, body, and soul as if it's wrapped up in a gold package with diamond-crusted ribbons. You are a delicate flower that is deserving of the water and sun that it needs.

- A man who is on a similar spiritual journey as you doesn't mean he's the one for you. It simply mean you both are on a similar journey

   I've made this mistake more than once. I had to learn the hard way that people who want the same things you want in life doesn't correlate to the perfect mate. Your journeys match, but your personalities may clash.

- **Let him lead**

   There's nothing wrong with letting a man know you're interested, but let him build up the courage to ask you out on that first date, and second, and third. Men love a challenge, because it brings a certain amount of mystery and intrigue about you. If you make it too easy for him, he may lose interest. Believe it or not, it's the quickest way to land us in the "friend zone". Yes, ladies, men have friend zones too, and for those who desire to be in a committed, loving relationship beware that you don't end up there.

- **Don't give too much of yourself too soon.** Not just with sex, but with details about your life. The first month of dating should be all about getting to know one another. That shouldn't include telling your new guy about Uncle Byron's drug problem, giving your ATM pin, or that you can't wait to put on that wedding dress you've purchased one year ago.

- **Don't force love**

  Forced love is never genuine love, so let it flourish naturally. Until then....self love should be sufficient enough.

  I revisit my guideline notes every now and then as a reminder. I'll be honest and tell you that it's a must, because when I fall in love, I fall fast and hard. It's a process for me in learning the importance of being happy with self without the presence of a man. That has a lot to do with me being a hopeless romantic, as well. I live for love stories about couples on how they first met and fell in love. I love those sappy movies with the happy endings.

When I get a sniff of love in the air,

I question why it hasn't happened for me,

yet. I understand now that these past few

years were utilized in a way for me to

discover my faults with men, therefore I

wasn't ready for a relationship like I

thought I was. The universe sent me each

guy as a lesson. These guys were my

teachers and they didn't even know it.

They've taught me what I don't need in a

relationship, and they've also taught me

what I deserve. Those problem

relationships that I've encountered

indicated that I had an addiction to

relationships.

Relationship addiction is much like

drug addiction. I didn't care about the

lasting effects that the toxic relationship would have on my already fragile heart. I needed a fix, even if it was temporary. Even when I knew it was a temporary fix, I kept at it, meaning I kept sleeping with him. The sex was fulfilling a void, but the energy that was being exchanged was depleting my self-esteem. I've read online that when you become intimate with someone, you receive the energy of that person that is thrusting into you.

That's why it's so important who you choose to become intimate with. If he complains a lot and embodies that of a hurt person with a hopeless attitude seventy-five percent of the time, chances are you will be too. No matter how happy you were when you met him, his negative feelings will be projected unto you. My last toxic relationship was proof. Me being a lover of love, he was the complete opposite, due to being hurt in the past. He was a self-proclaimed proud single person, but you could tell he really wanted to be in love. He confirmed how hurt he's been with conversations we've had. I looked past that and took a risk anyway. To make a long story short, I became intimate with him.

After the intimacy, all communication ceased. Needless to say, I became that same bitter person that he was, because I allowed him to treat me the way he was treated. That lasted for a short period of time, because I refused to let him see that I was misusing my energy. I refused to allow him to render me powerless with his hurt. As a result, I did what I had to do by moving on and in the end I won. I won, because my disappointment didn't turn into anger for him. Instead, I prayed for him and made peace with the fact that he was emotionally unstable and wasn't ready for the love that I was trying to give him.

The lesson in that relationship is that I should love someone who loves like I do. I didn't know that before, but the universe brought him to me to show me that.

I have fully recovered from my relationship addiction with the knowledge that I must become the best woman that I can possibly be before I become someone's significant other. Folks around me in great relationships are in great relationships, because it's their time. They've worked hard to get that type of relationship, and I understand that they'll have to work even harder to maintain it.

My time will come when I'm blessed with the man who God will send me, but until then I will work on me to become at peace with the way things are now as a single woman. The love I want will come to me naturally, but until then I will receive the love I need and that love is from Lakia. Loving myself include committing to letting go of self-criticism, self-doubt, and the ability to accept myself and know that I don't need a man in order to be fully happy. The result: generating more power and understanding that happiness is an inside job.

Chapter 5

"Money often costs too much"~ Ralph Waldo Emerson

As I've said earlier in Chapter 3, money is a powerful piece of paper. It has the power to not only alter your mood, but change your life. I know that money can't buy me happiness, but it definitely takes me out of a funk. That funk is the monetary forces in my life that drives me to effects of depression. The depression builds when I have to auction off which bill is more important to pay because of insufficient funds. It builds when I foresee all of the things I have to do for my publishing company in order for it and my authors to become successful. Having a lack of funds have come from many causes, but shortened hours at the employer was the main cause.

All of this was taking place while I was training myself to spend less and save more, and it wasn't easy. It wasn't easy until I noticed a change in the way I treat money. I will share with you my secrets on building a better financial nest. My disclaimer: I am in no way a financial planner, or any other professional financial expert. This is the Lakia way of how to make your money work for you, even if you don't make enough.

- **Open a bank account**

  I know you love the idea of saving money without the confines of bank fees and fear of overdrafts, but keeping your money in a shoe box is not the way to go. If you keep your money in a bank account, it will not only be much safer there, but it can build interest. Of course, you'll have to make sure you stay out of the negative, but even if it's five bucks every two weeks, you're building your nest.

- **If you have debt, work on paying it off**

  I am one to tell you that I was very selfish with my money with not paying off my debt. It took the lesson in knowing that I'm not able to get the house I'm trying to purchase, because of who I owe. Don't wait until the last minute as I have. Before you try to invest in something life changing as buying a home, pay off any remaining debt you have. Trust me, it will be a huge load off your shoulders, and you'll feel more confident in buying a home, car, or whatever huge purchase that requires good credit.

- **Treat your money like a plant**

  Add your water daily and your plant will grow. Much like your money, every little bit you add to your savings will help. Before you realize, you'll have more in your account than you'll expect.

- **Stick within your budget**

  I'm pretty sure that $6.00 bottle of laundry detergent works just as effectively as the one for $9.00. Oh! And they have cute stuff in thrift stores nowadays. Don't frown!

  Most importantly, thrifty fashions are easy on the pockets. All you need to do is know how to make them work with your sense of fashion. I've bought an entire outfit, including a pair of shoes for just under 20 bucks.

- **Distinguish the difference between what you need and what you want**

  I want to go to that show in Vegas, but I need to build my income. Vegas entertainers have money. I don't. That's pretty much self-explanatory.

To this day, I still follow my guidelines, and probably will for years to come. Having better financial stability is a priority for me, hence my reasons why I haven't purchased a home, yet. There are a lot of responsibilities to being a home owner, and before I make that type of investment, I want to make sure I'm capable of handling one financially. The last thing I want is to purchase a home, only to go into foreclosure a year later. So, I'm stepping out on optimism and seeing the glass half full on this opportunity. When I hear the words "Congratulations, you're a home owner!" I will have accomplished another life- long goal of mine. Until then, I will continue to make my money work for me. I will make my money work for me in ways when even if my next paycheck isn't enough, I'll still feel financially comfortable.

Overall, I've learned that money is very tricky. You have to know how to use it, know when to use it, recognize what you need, and forget what you want. My lesson: I'm learning to use my money wisely by getting what I need, instead of getting what I want. The only thing I should WANT is financial freedom. I'll be honest and share that I'll get that cute little dress I see hanging in my favorite store on occasion. It's called paying yourself first.

However, I know not to go overboard and spend excessively. I hate those feelings I get after spending majority of my paycheck. I don't want to experience those feelings anymore. It's called buyer's remorse and it's mixed feelings of guilt, irresponsibility, and hopelessness all wrapped up into a ball; a ball that hits me right in the gut. Instead of those feelings, I aim to feel a ball of responsibility, pride, satisfaction, and accomplishment every time money lands in my hand.

Chapter 6

"Love yourself, instead of abusing yourself."~Karolina Kurkova

I t has taken me a long time to understand the true meaning of loving myself. I used to ask myself what does someone do to love themselves? Does it mean to take myself out on a date? Does it mean to treat myself to a gift? Does it mean to visit my favorite nail shop and get a mani/pedi? The answer to all of those questions is YES. However, loving yourself comes in many different forms. I've come to discover that loving yourself also requires internal rehabilitation which is more important. Your heart and soul that was damaged from past relationships must be fixed before anything else, and that is YOUR responsibility, no one else's. The problem that I had was looking for others to heal me from my pain, when in fact that's MY responsibility. Not my friends, my mother, or my lover.

Sometimes, I ask myself why I didn't understand that before. That's because I thought it was THEIR responsibility, because of the role that these people have in my life. My strength was validated by my mother who raised me as the person I am today, the advice from friends helped me to understand a lot more about men, and my lover who was responsible for bringing me happiness. I've realized that all of those things had a lot to do with Lakia. My mom did raise me the best way she could, and I must say without being biased--I turned out to be great! My mother influenced a lot of my decisions however; most of my strength comes from my own choices in how I choose to live life. With such arduous moments I've had to endure in my life, I could've made the choice to give up on a lot of shit and just let things fall apart, but I didn't want that.

It is my decision to not become detrimental to self that gives me strength. It's also looking at how things could be if I didn't change, or try hard enough, or stay optimistic that has also kept me from turning into another direction. As one of my sister girlfriends say…the quality of your life depends on the quality of your choices.

Today, I am still learning to love myself more, starting with internal rehab. It begins with trying to shed the pounds from years of emotional eating. Eating was my addiction, and my defense mechanism from feeling stress that was due to whatever wasn't going right in my life. I looked to food as my comforter without realizing that I was hurting myself even more.

As a result, daily exercise and trying to eat right is high on my list of "must dos". My internal rehab also includes healing self from past relationships. A lot of what I required in relationships was non-existent, because I wasn't giving myself those same requirements. When I learned that, it was such a hard pill to swallow. However, I accept what I've done with these relationships and use them as motivation to become better, and understand that I have to mirror what I want from others. If I want love, I have to have it for myself first. If I want respect, I'll have to have respect for myself first.

Learning and OVERstanding were my initial steps towards healing self, followed with the understanding that I am responsible for my own happiness. Never depend on others to give you happiness or increase your peace. When you do, you set yourself up for emotional failure, which could lead to depression. Instead of taking responsibility, you'll blame others for how badly you feel. Take matters into your own hands by claiming your thoughts, emotions, and actions as your own. Knowing all of this has helped heal my heart, and that ladies and gentlemen, is a part of internal rehabilitation.

Personal acceptance was something else I've dealt with. I didn't always accept my dark skin, as I have struggled with it mostly in my early to mid teens. Back in the late eighties and early nineties, light skin black folks were considered the most attractive among African-Americans. It was clearly evident in media and entertainment, which in turn convinced my impressionable peers, including me. I believed that light skin was "in", because for one I didn't have a "LuPita Nyong'o" to look up to. Secondly, all the little boys I had crushes on, had crushes on my light skinned classmates, and lastly I was called every un-appealing, disparaging, and derogatory name related to being dark skinned that you could think of including "darkie", "midnight", "blacky", "tar-baby", and "spook". A boy even called me a dinosaur to my face once, but I have no idea if that had anything to do with my skin or my looks, maybe both.

As a young teen going through changes, it definitely did a number on my self-esteem. As a result, I felt unattractive to the point where approaching boys I liked was something I could not do. While in my late teens, I dressed like a boy to prevent my curves from showing. I didn't want any attention from boys, not even while wearing a pair of fitted jeans. If I did wear fitted jeans, I'd rock an oversized shirt to cover my butt. However, wearing the big clothes didn't last for too long. It took a while for me to embrace the fact that I had become a woman with womanly curves

Once I did, all of the baggy clothes were put to the back of the closet. I started dressing more feminine and even carried myself more like a lady. Wearing baggy clothes made me walk differently. Once I changed my wardrobe, I began to walk with more confidence and had more pep in my step. I even felt "pretty" despite my challenge to accept my dark skin. Soon after my wardrobe change, I dug deep down into my soul to find the true beauty within me.

It was important for me to go further than skin deep to find why I really am beautiful, no matter what shade I am. It was important for me to go deeper than skin-deep to understand that what all of the little boys and the little girls in school said about me weren't true. My soul revealed that my being is perfect just the way it is, because God made me. When God made me, he didn't make any mistakes, so when I'm called "ugly", it usually comes from people with ugly personalities. People with ugly personalities usually show that ugly side externally which reveals more as they become older.

At the age of twenty-one, I've realized that when I was told I was black and ugly, they really meant that I was dark and lovely. I forgave those kids who told me that I was black and ugly, because they were in fact just kids. Kids are cruel, and in some cases, they grow to become destructive adults. I forgave them all and I prayed for them in that they have become productive and respectable adults today. As far as relationships today, I no longer look for them. I've come to understand that things like love and relationships will come naturally and will come around when you least expect.

I'm currently single, but instead of pining over a man and whining over not being in a relationship, I use my freedom for personal growth. I've also learned to accept no less than what I truly deserve, and what I deserve is love, peace, happiness, respect, equality, understanding, and joy. The good thing is I've already given myself what I deserve. However, having someone who adds to all of those is extra sweet. I am worthy of him.

In the meantime, I stay content with where I am right now. I am giving myself understanding in knowing that it's okay to be me and with all of my flaws. I'm not perfect. In fact, I'm perfectly imperfect. I find joy in knowing that as long as I have breath in my body, I'm capable of achieving greatness. I find equality in knowing my strengths and weaknesses. I find peace in knowing that it's okay to make mistakes, because we learn from them. I find happiness in knowing how to live with everything I don't have, instead of focusing on why I don't have everything I want...in due time, is what I remind myself. I find peace in knowing that my opportunities are limitless. I find respect whenever I choose what I'm deserving of.

Chapter 7

"Motherhood is...difficult...and rewarding."~
Gloria Estefan

M otherhood is a full time job that can be stressful, yet rewarding. As my son and daughter get older, I see their personalities flourish. I am proud of the people they are growing to be. I pray they grow into adulthood and continue to flourish into productive and respectable people. I guess I am a good mother, despite what their father used to say to me towards the end of our relationship.

Because of me calling it quits in the relationship which was full of turmoil, I was deemed a bad mother. I was also told that I was being selfish, because I was "splitting up the family". There's one thing he said that sticks to me, and that was I'd never find another man to be with me, because I had kids with him.

I can't remember what my response was word from word, but I remember having to remind him that he was only trying to discourage me from seeing other men, which I can now understand. When you still have hope for a relationship, you say just about anything in anger. Their father telling me that I was a bad mother affected me, even though I've tried not to let it. He used to be extremely picky with little things regarding the kids that he didn't approve of, trying to prove that I'm not a good mother. For example, my daughter has thick, natural hair that was kept in ponytails. As mothers, we know how little girls' hair doesn't stay in place or "neat" all day.

When their dad picked them up from school and saw that her hair wasn't neat, he blamed me by saying that I don't do her hair correctly and in a matter that was pleasing to him. His pickiness used to hurt me terribly, and he knew that it would. His actions caused more strain between us as co-parenting. It had gotten so bad, that I didn't even want him involved with his kids. That thought didn't last for too long. I am one to tell you that having a father in your life matters.

As someone who has lost a father at an early age, I know how it is to grow up without one. My children's father is living, and he wants to be there for them. I can't let what he used to say to me affect their relationship. As a result from the pickiness, I sometimes make extreme efforts to prove how much of a good mother I am. Honestly, I have no one to prove, but myself.

During one Christmas, I've spent my entire paycheck on gifts and a nice size tree for the kids to find them under. That paycheck was supposed to go to rent. Needless to say, I've lost that house which is why I'm currently looking for another. It was one of those experiences where I felt like I had to prove to their dad (and myself) that I'm a good mother. I had no rent money, but my children had the Christmas they wanted.

Besides the occasional need for a reliable sitter, dating and motherhood never really became an issue for me. The men I've dated had no problem with me being a mother, especially the men that are parents themselves. If I ever come across one that actually does have a problem, he can kick rocks! I've been very careful with my children NOT meeting the men I've dated. I've even made it aware to their father that they will not meet any guy that I date, unless we BOTH make it official. As of now, I choose not to date for various reasons. My main reason is focusing more on my career as a writer.

I'll be honest and share that I miss the company of a man on occasion, but as a woman who is going through emotional recovery it's in my best interest to not entertain a man at this time. That is a part of the journey to loving myself more. It's not wise for me to hook up with a man right now simply because I miss the presence of one. I wouldn't be fair to him, and I wouldn't be fair to myself.

Going out with friends was difficult in a sense that I felt like I should be home with my kids, instead of at some loud place, putting in work on the dance floor. I've mentioned this to one of my girlfriends who I feel tends to know me more than I know myself, sometimes. She asked if feeling guilty was a result of losing

Robert. When she asked that, I felt an immediate sense of relief. It made perfect sense since I've been having that guilty conscience since Robert transitioned.

I felt relief in finally knowing that I'm not really a bad mother whose priorities are fucked up. I felt relief in knowing that I deserve to have fun in life, and just because I'm a mother, it doesn't mean I need to stay locked in the house. I've come to the conclusion with this lesson: having and raising kids shouldn't BE your life, but an added bonus to your life.

Overall, I'm not trying to be the "perfect" parent that I thought I had to be. Instead, I'm being a REAL parent. I'm a mother who understands that I was a woman before I became a mom, and I shouldn't feel guilty for wanting to be around other adults, sometimes. Trust when I say that you'd want to spend some quality time with your friends, or even some time by yourself. It's your way of staying sane, because if you're around your children all day or all the time, it'll drive you NUTS! As a mother, you owe it to yourself to spend quality time with like-minded adults or even better, yourself at least two days out of the week.

If you're fortunate enough to have free time on the weekends, take advantage of it by going places that doesn't involve children. Get a reliable sitter even if you have no place to go. You can use the quiet time to recuperate, because parenting is a full time job. Other jobs are required to make their employees take breaks, because they need that down time to re-energize. The same goes for parents, or you will not function well as one. It's very necessary to spend some portion of your life having fun outside of motherhood. It's all about creating that balance for yourself by setting aside some time for self-sufficiency that is pertinent to your peace of mind.

Chapter 8

"There is nothing more beautiful than seeing a person be themselves. Imagine going through your day being unapologetically you."~ Steve Maraboli

B eing my true self was another struggle of mine for quite some time. It's also brought me some clarity to why I used to give too much of myself too soon with men, only to feel empty in the end.

Once I've done that, I felt like I had nothing else to offer. I've failed to see the never-ending fierceness within myself, so I did what any insecure person would do. I sat back and observed other folks that seemed to "do it" so well; whatever "it" was. I came to the conclusion that I wasn't good enough for the guys I approached and in the meantime, I doubted myself more and more.

There were times when I actually downplayed my awesomeness, so I could get attention from a man that I had interest in. Looking back now, I was a woman who did not have high self-esteem. Another problem I had was being a "people pleaser". There's nothing wrong with pleasing others but in my case, it was out of manipulation instead of genuine generosity. I used to go out of my way for folks (men in particular) so that I would be liked or adored as much as friends or folks they've genuinely cared for.

It all stemmed from caring what people thought of me. After much personal evaluation, I came to understand that I wasn't being my true self. What you give in any relationship you encounter should be reciprocated. It never worked that way for me, because I was either giving too much too soon or not giving enough. I had a hard time balancing both. I've discovered that "studying" others would never work, because they're not me and I'm not them. With the exception of females having a similar name as mine, I'm the only Lakia in this world and now I'm giving you the best version of Lakia that I can be and I'm okay with that. I'm okay with the person I am today, and any friend who is genuine would be okay with me, too. During a self-evaluation, I asked myself how I could balance the act of giving without compromising my love for self and without feeling empty afterwards. My lesson in this: I've rid the fear of just being my honest self. I've also stopped comparing myself to others. We are all unique in our own way, and I refuse to be a "carbon copy" of someone else.

It's never worth going into a personal tug of war just to be liked or adored. People like different people for different reasons. I had to realize that just because I wasn't getting enough attention from "someone", it doesn't make me any less intelligent, pretty, kind, thoughtful, and fun to be around. I know I'm all those and if someone fails to see that, then the person is not worth my time and I'll be okay with that.

Part of my journey to not giving too much of myself too soon involves my vagina. This challenge is also the reason why I've put dating on hold, as I've mentioned earlier. As I currently learn how to navigate through this life without a significant other, I find it difficult to connect with men who I find attractive, without taking it further before getting to know his favorite color, what foods he likes to eat, his likes, his dislikes, his passion for life, and things of that nature.

My past dealings with men barely ended on a good note, HENCE the key word "end". Taking it further without really getting to know a man and not knowing his intentions for me was a mistake I've made more than once, so I've made a promise that the next time I'd meet a man, I'd take my time with him and move slowly. As a woman who strives to find that someone special who is equally interested in my mind as he is with my ass, I've realized that my quest to find that man appears to be coming to a dead end. My last encounter has given me much more insight on how resilient and dedicated I am to keeping my promise. Want to know what my promise is? The answer is to take my time with him before I give all of me.

I'm at a place in my life where I'm no longer playing around with these ninjas! At the same time, I'm putting myself in check and I constantly remind myself, as I say "Self, your vagina is valuable. It's like fine wine that tastes better with time. If that wine is opened to soon, it will not be as good as it could be if you wait to open it." My vagina is attached to a woman who absolutely loves sex. I have a very high sex drive, so I'd love to have it, except I'm not in a hurry. Future guy, I want to get to know who are. What you need (besides booty), and what you desire in life. I want to know if the chemistry I feel with you is mutual and will remain.

I consider myself an interesting enough lady to get to know on a deeper level, and I find intellectual conversation to be more stimulating than sexual penetration. Although sex is enjoyable, it's more enjoyable when you're in love. If a guy cannot put forth effort into getting to know more of me, but every other conversation I have with him is trying to tempt me into bed, then he isn't ready, willing, and probably isn't that much into me.

I get it now, and this time a man's verbal seduction will not be as effective as it used to be on me. I've been getting better at reading between the lines, and decoding bullshit when I hear it. I'm not proud of the choices I've made in the past regarding men. However, I know that those are lessons I've had to learn in order to be much wiser. I know what I want and I know what I deserve. I also know that I'm worth the wait. If I choose to sleep with a guy, it will be because I find that he deserves it. I'm also putting myself in a position where I could also get hurt, and/or disappointed, which is a risk with my fragile heart.

If I trust him with my heart by giving him my body, it says a lot. Something as serious as that should be considered, because I feel that he deserves it. Let's make it clear that I would put it on him like he's the only man on earth! I am confident about that! I'm confident about that! However, my confidence lacks when I feel that a guy is interested too soon in sex, because it tells me that I'm not interesting enough to get to know on a deeper level. I want a shirt that says "I am MORE than my vagina".

I am MORE than my vagina!

I am a warrior of life!

I've been through some things, and yet. I'm still standing!

I have wants, dreams, needs, desires that involves my family, friends, and my lover I have yet to meet

I am ambitious!

I am complicated, but if you're willing to figure me out without hesitation, you're alright with me.

I'd play Xbox with you!

I can be silly at times!

Those are just a few things about me that I want people to know.

When I'm interested in a guy, I try to invest as much time as I can to discover what kind a person he is. I think that's important for anyone to do if they plan to take things to the next level physically.

To my future lover, whoever it will be.... Please take me seriously. When I invest time in getting to know you, I do it wholeheartedly. The sex will come in due time. Get to know me first. I'd love to get to know you. Only then will I'll never mind to make plans with you, because you've proven that sex is not your only intentions for me.

I'm not saying I'm looking for a husband. I stopped looking a long time ago. However, when the opportunity presents itself to meet a guy who I deem interesting enough in getting to know, I'd at least like to know that giving him some of my energy is the right thing to do.

My past "situationships" have taught me a lot of good, bad, and indifferences with men, as well as myself. While I instill these lessons in saving my vagina for the right guy, I'll wait for the day when I meet a guy who will see so much in me that my vagina is actually the last thing on his mind when we connect. That right there is great chemistry. I'm rebuilding my energy, and I'm valuing my body.

Being the best version of me has been a priority of mine for some time and since I've started this journey, I've become aware of the positive changes within me. Things that would usually bother me, no longer bother me. I've learned to accept folks for who they are and not for what I'd want them to be. However, the biggest lesson that I have learned from this continuing journey to self-improvement is that in order to love myself unconditionally, I have to value my failures and mistakes.

Without them, I could never grow. Without failures, I'll never know what it feels like to rise to the top. I call my failures and mistakes lessons. Each lesson I've learned has taught me something, whether it's something I need to do or something I need to stop doing. Each lesson is like a stair step, meaning each step that I'm taking is leading me one step closer to growth and personal evolution.

Yesterday, I was emotionally sick. I was confused about what I want and what I need to be. I was also a people pleaser, meaning my mentality was "fuck my life, but as long as you're happy!" Today, my emotional health has improved with the knowledge and understanding that being SELFish is sometimes necessary. My today will create change, therefore preparing me for a much different tomorrow, as I learn something new about myself every day. I'm progressing, and what you see now is a lot better version of Lakia than a year ago.

Chapter 9

"Often, our perceptions can be a hindrance to our

success."~ Jordan Blake Michiels

I used to think that outside sources hindered me from becoming who or what I want to be in life, until I looked in the mirror one day and saw a woman who has been in her own way for a very long time. I could blame my job for taking up most of my time for not enough money. I could blame lack of inspiration for my writer's block that I often get. I could even blame all the guys who have caused my heart to become fragile. I choose not to blame anyone or any challenge, as I have taken responsibility in my decision making. I made the choice to stay at this job. I've made the choice to write this book, and I've made the choice to deal with these guys.

However, the aforementioned shouldn't hinder me from becoming great, unless I allow them. Unfortunately, there was one difficult decision I've made that has significantly impacted me emotionally. It involved a lot of frustration, tears, and overall trepidation on my part.

If you know me personally, you know that I'm real big on friendship, support, loyalty, and sisterhood. So when one of my sister girlfriends offered me an opportunity of my lifetime, I didn't hesitate to say yes, because what she offered sound like it would be submerged in nothing but friendship, support, loyalty, and sisterhood. She offered me a part as co- host of an online radio show with our other girlfriends.

For me, it was an opportunity waiting to happen, because throughout my life, I've wondered how I would fit in the communications/radio world. I even thought about going to school for mass communications, but obviously that never happened. The upside to this opportunity was being a part of something that represented what I am. I consider myself to be loving, supportive, a great listener, a good conversationalist, etc. It also gave me the clarity that I can be more expressive and not worry about what folks would think of me. I even became more aware and knowledgeable about men and relationships from co hosting a radio show with my girlfriends.

There was nothing like having girl talk every week, and allowing the people to listen to us. It made me feel like I have become a part of something great. The downside to this was the more popular we became, the less significant I felt as a co-host. At one point, I was told I had a "background personality", which took me by surprise. From that point on, the pressure to be "perfect" was heavy on the brain, especially since there were concerns of opening up, and inadequate written and speaking communication on my part. It all began to do a number on my confidence not only with co-hosting, but as Lakia Nichole, the brand.

The process of being myself included trying to absorb qualities from the other co-hosts, so that I could evolve from the background personality that I've apparently adopted. One co-host provided humor, so I tried to be funny like her. One was spiritual, so I try to be as spiritual as her. One is sexy, so I try to match my sexiness with hers, and one spoke with much eloquence and intelligence, so I try to speak as eloquently as her.

That often led to me being selectively opinionated, which in turn did not help sometimes. In fact, being selective in what I wanted to say made the situation worse, because I ended up struggling with what I wanted to convey. Needless to say, something I wanted to remain a part of badly was hindering my confidence to the point that I became frustrated.

I became frustrated with myself, because as much as I've tried to better my public speaking, my written communication skills, and even my personality, it all just wasn't working for me. The initial sign of my hosting incapability sparked doubt, and that doubt grew as the show's popularity grew. As a result, I made the regretful, but necessary decision to depart from the show. This decision has revealed that underlying issue I've had with not accepting myself for what I truly am and what I'm capable of doing.

The lesson in all of this is that I have to love what I believe and believe what I love. I no longer believed that I could evolve from my struggles within the group, and I didn't want to be responsible for detracting from the show's brand in any way, shape, or form. I did what I felt I had to do for the girls, as well as myself.

I took time away to work on Lakia from the inside out. I wanted to regain my confidence by studying my craft as a writer and taking it more seriously. I even took in some time to dive into some more passions of mine like taking up a modern dance class. I must say that being a part of the radio/podcast show for two years has allowed me to come out of my shell, and for that I am grateful. It has opened my eyes for me to see that I have been a hindrance to myself and as a result, I'm more opened to doing events as Lakia Nichole. The time away has also encouraged me to get out of my own way and accomplish my personal goals.

Another lesson I've learned from this is that I have to love myself for who I am from the inside out. If you focus on being a carbon copy of someone else, you'll never know how fierce you really are. My problem was trying to use everyone else's water and sun to help my plant grow, when I have plenty of my own water and sun. My hindrance was caring too much about how folks viewed me among my co-hosts.

Unfortunately, my hindrance trickled outside of the show and into my personal space. I've always cared about what others thought of me, but since the show it became quite severe to the point that I didn't want to be the quiet and reserved Lakia anymore. I wanted to be more outspoken, sassy, funny, and more socially aware. I was playing Tug-Of-War with myself, as a result.

I'm still working on breaking this habit by constantly reminding myself that I am great just the way I am. I don't speak a lot on politics and religion, because there's a lot I need to learn on both subjects. I don't speak much on socialism and won't cry every time I pick up a newspaper, but that doesn't mean I don't care. I won't spend a ton on beauty products, because I'm low maintenance and proud of it. My beauty radiates from the inside, and that includes some psychological and spiritual tips that I've adopted for me to understand that.

I'm learning to show more confidence in my own skin. I'm focusing more on what I do have, instead of what I don't have. I'm embracing the qualities I possess and understanding that whatever qualities I don't have and/or lacking, I can improve. I'm also learning to leave competition out of beauty. I'm competing with no one but myself, and I do that with purchasing a new outfit, or just simply inventing a new hairstyle.

Overall, I'm channeling my energy into a new and positive direction. I no longer extensively care what others think of me and as a result, I've become more comfortable with the Lakia I really am. There's a quote by Author Steve Maraboli and he says *"There's nothing more rare, nor more beautiful, than a woman being unapologetically herself; Comfortable in her perfect imperfection. To me, that is the true essence of beauty."* I couldn't agree more with this quote.

My imperfections are what make me human. I'm more beautiful because I acknowledge my imperfections and work around them. Perfection is the grandest illusion that the universe have adopted. When we as humans believe that the imperfections we have are not inadequacies, but reminders that we have capabilities, strength, and courage to better them. Better them NOT to perfection, but good enough for the person that you are. Sometimes, we lose ourselves in the things we love, but we find ourselves there, as well. The girls and the show helped me to lose myself, but I've discovered myself, as well. For that, I am forever thankful.

Chapter 10

"One of the most beautiful qualities of true friendship is to understand and to be understood,"~ Lucius Annaeus Seneca

True friendship is such a blessing in a way that the persons whom you consider genuine friends will be the persons to never steer you in the wrong direction. These loyal people in your life will tell you like it is even if it hurts, because they really love you. What your family members don't have your true friends will. I'm blessed to have a few women that fit the description of true friends.

When I was in my twenties, I used to correlate being worthy of friendship with how many friends you have. At my age now, the only thing that matters to me is the quality of the friendships I have, instead of the quantity. Unfortunately for me, there's a thin line between being friendly and being a people pleaser. I'm learning to not be a "yes" type of friend, or a friend who'll agree with just about anything out of fear of starting arguments, and other ramifications that would lead to broken friendships.

I'm learning to trust the process when it comes to friendships. You'll know true friendship exists in the universe when it'll allow those to be as expressive as they need to be without fear of hurting others. I'm learning that it's okay to disagree with your friends about anything.

If it is a true friendship, the bond is unbreakable. Therefore, the strong bond will not allow a disagreement to become more than just that. I'm also learning that true friends will even criticize you, but out of love. That's simply constructive criticism, and learning the difference between constructive and exaggerated criticism is important. Accepting constructive criticism from friends is a much bigger pill to swallow, as opposed to getting it from strangers.

For me, I used to think it was a step away from being unsupportive. When I was a part of the radio show, it was difficult for me to accept that there were concerns of my skills in written and speaking communication. I was what you would say "in my feelings". Fortunately, that didn't last too long, as I've taken responsibility in studying self. That includes learning what my weaknesses and strengths are within my craft. That also includes doing things to strengthen my weaknesses in my craft. Because of my friends' constructive criticism, I take my craft a lot more seriously.

The great thing about having true friends is the understanding that they have of you. My friends understand why it was necessary to leave the show, and that makes the wound heal a little faster. I appreciate each and every one of them for standing by me and supporting me for leaving, so I can accomplish my goals. I hope they know I would do the same for them.

Friends are a blessing to have in so many ways. Friends know your flaws, but love you anyways. Most importantly, they show their support not only during a time of happiness, but during times of trouble. Whether you want to believe it or not, friends make life much more exciting, fulfilling, and full of joy. If your friends bring the opposite of excitement, fulfillment, and joy in your life, it's really time to evaluate some people, including yourself.

Chapter 11

"Dickmatized is being hypnotized by the DICK...I realize I have been dickmatized in the past, by choice,"~ Jill Scott

N ow that I've shared how I'm learning the steps to evolving into the Lakia Nichole I'm supposed to be, let me share how I'm coping with these changes, particularly sex. As I go through celibacy for the third time, it's becoming clear to me that my biggest weakness is penis. I mean, not just any penis, but that good penis that some women just can't shake. Good penis is usually attached to the most emotionally unstable man or worse, a penis that is attached to an unavailable man that have absolutely no business putting his good penis inside of us.

Unfortunately, we allow it because we've simply become dickmatized. Dickmatization will have us doing things we wouldn't normally do like stalk his social media profiles, become extra possessive, or become his woman without his knowledge or permission and that may all occur after the first sexual encounter. Our experience with being dickmatized comes with the lesson that good dick comes with a price that'll cost you your dignity. Some of us may not care enough about the emotional instability of the man that the dick is attached to, because we're stuck on how good the dick makes us feel. Then we blame the guys, because we feel they "play too many games".

We tolerate a lot of shit, because we don't want to let that good dick go, hoping he'll change. I've been dickmatized several times throughout my life and learned the hard way that you'll never be taken seriously if you've given up the vagina too soon. Good dick doesn't always have to be attached to emotionally unstable men. Some men just like to bone with no strings attached, and that's okay, especially if he's honest about his intentions in the beginning of the relationship. Unfortunately, we as women who are looking to commit will think our vagina will be good enough to make him change his ways. I've done that, and that shit doesn't work.

TRUST! You can have the best *Harlem Nights* Sunshine type of vagina, but a man will NEVER commit, if he's not ready. Your cookie is no different from the other cookies he keeps in his cookie jar. Don't expect to be taken out either if you've already given up the vagina too soon. You've already established a certain parameter that he's going to get accustomed to, so he'll feel like taking you out on dates that you deserve will be a waste of time. Meanwhile, he's taking someone else that he hasn't smashed yet to some exotic location and you're still trying to get a movie date. Suffering from dickmatization can be a mutha! Celibacy is necessary for me to practice, because I loathe the feelings I get when being dickmatized. They're feelings of being undignified, being lonely, and the feeling of worthlessness. I'm coping with penis withdrawal better than I thought I would. I do have my days (or nights) when I have urges that will have my uterus doing flips. However, I remain cool with being penis-free.

These penis-free days have helped me see things more clearly. I'm also more aware of what I deserve in a relationship, and what I'm worthy of. I even find myself taking more of a spiritual path. I'm re-building my self-esteem, setting boundaries, and lowering my expectations so whenever I meet HIM, he and I will know of each other's intentions within the relationship. I'm also learning to distinguish the difference between what I need and what I want from a man. Unfortunately, I get confused thinking I need penis. I shall change. I'm a work in progress.

Chapter 12

"Go confidently in the direction of your dreams. Live the life you have imagined."~ Henry David Thoreau

I had an epiphany some time ago, that has truly given me a new outlook on my accomplishments. I've discovered how lazy I became with studying my craft, and letting fear consume me with negative thoughts and doubts about running my publishing company. The epiphany came to me while working the nine to five, and it finally dawned on me why I was no longer happy doing what I was doing.

While working as a corporate slave, I wasn't taking time and the energy to invest in my business as a publisher and writer. I was putting my company on hold because I was letting my nine to five take over my life. I realized that if I could project that of a hard worker for these corporate folks, then I could project that of a hard-working publisher, and getting my business off the ground. I told myself that it was time to stop bullshitting around and work harder towards my dreams.

I developed a thicker skin for any nay-sayers and doubters that might come my way, and rid myself of the negative thoughts and self-doubting. I gathered loads of motivation to reignite the passion I once had. Anything that would distract me from writing I had no time for, and I started coming up with story ideas left and right. I even re-launched the website to my publishing company with the acceptance of submissions, as opposed to before when fear of failure kept me from accepting submissions from aspiring authors.

The lesson here; If you want something badly, you'll do everything you can to get it. I want stability and success with my publishing company, so that's what I'm striving for. I've gotten out of my own way, and I'm making good use of my energy by investing into my goals. Since I've taken the initiative to work on my company, the universe has been pulling me in the right direction.

Taking this direction has shown me where I went wrong when I originally launched my publishing company. I didn't put forth effort in marketing, promotion, and basically getting my name and my company's name out there. I used the internet exclusively to spread the word about everything. I was too lazy to pound the pavement, too cheap to rent a book signing table at an event, and was too much of an introvert to go out and network.

Now that I have the opportunity, the time, the commitment, and more knowledge of running an independent publishing company, I feel more secure, able, and ready. It's been non-stop work since my epiphany at work, and every step I take as a publisher is one step closer to accomplishing my goal to stability and success. I'm not where I want to be, but if I keep doing what I'm doing, I will get there...maybe sooner than later.

I wish this epiphany I've had come to me earlier than it did, or maybe it has and I didn't see it because fear was blinding me. It has unfortunately proven that fear took over a lot of my decision making. I don't want to say that I've wasted time, because each experience has taught me a valuable lesson. It's the reason for why I'm where I am today, so I appreciate knowing that my time was never wasted. I think the thing that really kept me going was the fact that I've never stopped believing in myself.

I've had doubts, but my belief in knowing I could make it outweighed any doubts I've had. Folks like Michael Jordan, Oprah, and J.K Rowling were told "no" before they became who they are today. They never gave up and their outcome is proof that nay-sayers don't have the final say in your goals. Most importantly, they've gotten out of their own way to accomplish their goals.

Chapter 13

"Sometimes, you like to let the hair do the talking!"~ James Brown

I've always had long hair until I did the big chop in 2011. For those who do not know the term "big chop", it's when a woman grows enough of her roots to the point where she'll cut off the remaining portion of her hair that's chemically straightened. Cutting my hair was such a liberating move, because I felt as if I didn't have to hide behind my long hair anymore.

Throughout middle and high school when my self-esteem suffered, I used my long hair as a crutch to convict some level of attractiveness. I didn't know any better, so of course my mindset was "If I'm not going to be an attractive adult, I'll at least have nice hair."

As a dark-skinned girl who was self-conscious about her skin, growing into adulthood was an even more emotional struggle. In my early twenties, I was slowly accepting the color of my skin, but the emotional attachment to my hair was still in effect. My long permanently straightened hair was precious to me.

It was my crowning glory that made me feel beautiful, even with the most basic hairstyle. Leaving the salon, I felt even more like a beautiful woman. Whether the fresh dew was a bun, a wrap, twists, etc. It always made me feel brand new, so trips to the salon every two weeks was important to me.

I couldn't fathom the thought of cutting my hair at all, because without it I'd be an ugly duckling, instead of a beautiful swan, or so I thought. It wasn't until years later while in my late thirties when I realized I didn't need long hair to feel "pretty". While on my pursuit to loving myself, I began to feel more accepting of myself. It didn't matter if my hair was long or short. I decided to cut my hair in order to feel a release. I was cutting away the weight from past insecurities, self-inflicted emotional wounds, and self-criticism.

After getting my hair cut extremely short I felt free, liberated, and even without hair I still felt like a brand new woman. I smiled and breathed a sigh of relief after taking my first look in the mirror as a short natural-haired woman. I still wore the same smile, the same set of eyes, and the same color skin. Nothing about me changed except my confidence which grew from that moment on. Oddly enough, I felt sexier with my new short hair.

As I rubbed my fingers through my tresses, embracing the shape of my head and loving the thickness of my curls, I came to the conclusion that I was pretty darn good-looking my whole life. I didn't need my hair to "feel" pretty, because I am. The verbal poison that I was accustomed to during most of my childhood sickened my young mind and my esteem weakened as a result. Feeling unattractive for most of my young life caused a lot of emotional wounds, but they've all healed.

Today, I still feel that same level of confidence, and as my hair grows longer, my pride as a dark-skinned black woman grows stronger. I now talk with sass, and my walk is fierce, as I sashay across any room with my head held high. Sometimes, you can't get me to shut up about how fine I am. I don't mean to sound vain, but for what I believed in my teens and as a young woman coming into her own in her twenties, expressing slight vanity is appropriate.

What I'm most proud of is that I didn't let the teasing affect me to the point that I became bitter and mean. It was never in my spirit to be a bully, because I know how hurtful it can feel. Some folks who were bullied in school grow to become bullies as adults. It's particularly why females are given the perception that they can't get along with each other, or that black men are perceived as "angry". I guarantee if you dig into the soul of the woman you can't "get along with" and that angry black man you might see and feel their hurt instead of anger.

Once the beauty radiates from your soul, it reflects your external beauty. In conclusion to this chapter, your beauty will never be defined by the amount of hair you have or even lack thereof. How you feel about yourself on the inside will radiate so brightly on the outside, you will be as beautiful as the full moon appearing from the clouds in the night sky.

Chapter 14

"Part of the reason that men seem so much less loving than women is that men's behavior is measured with a feminine ruler."~Francesca M. Cancian

I love men.

Men are one of the most beautiful creatures on earth, so it's only natural for me to want to attract them. I think about the list of men I used to date, and I can honestly say that any other woman would be impressed. Some were goal-oriented, a few had model good looks, and the rest were either great fathers, ambitious, and all had great personalities. The question is if they were all of those things, then why didn't it work out with any of them?

I've taken a look back and evaluated each relationship I've encountered to figure out why I was the common denominator for why they've all failed. Simply put...I was too eager to be committed, instead of taking the time to really get to know these men. My intention was to be someone's girlfriend. I wasn't focused on just having fun and casually dating. Thinking about it now, I was in no position to be committed to anyone because after my children's father, I needed to get my life back in order. I didn't see that back then, because all I wanted was a boo thing. It stems from what we were taught as little girls from the women in our families and from society.

Women were conditioned to believe that we had to be married by a certain age, and if we don't make the deadline, we are doomed to be single forever. Well, with that kind of pressure, I was determined not to be doomed by age of twenty-eight. I'm almost forty years old, and I obviously never made it to the altar. After my broken engagement with my children's father, I accepted the fact that walking down the aisle might not happen soon enough, but I still wanted that "Gina and Martin" type of relationship.

Each man I became involved with I approached with the idea of longevity. I was too fixated on building a future with him instead of just enjoying the "right now" with him. It took a long time for me to understand that I was rushing love, and I wasn't being genuine. I did some soul searching and discovered that it was really my fault for assuming they've all wanted what I wanted, even the ones who told me from the beginning that their intentions for me weren't similar to mine. I'm now learning to accept their honesty, and never assume that they want more. Communication with men is different now, as opposed to before. Before, what men used to tell me was actually twisted around in my mind to make it sound like something I wanted to hear. Today, what they tell me is THEIR words from their mouths, and not my imagination convincing me otherwise.

I'm a self-proclaimed bullshit decoder now, thanks to the experiences I've had with men. Talks with girlfriends and self-help books like "He's Just Not That Into You." have helped too. I can read between the lines, and pick up on what he's avoiding to say. I'm learning to trust more of my intuition, which never fails me. Because of all of the new communication skills, communication with men is a lot better now. I can carefully weed out opportunists from the ones who want a genuine friendship. I'm also a lot more patient and that really helps.

I've come to the conclusion that love need to come naturally, and I will find my soul mate wherever he is and whenever God reveals. If I ever get married that would be great, and if I never get married, I'll be okay. As you can see, I'm still single…and guess what? No doom has taken place. I'm good.

Chapter 15

A really strong woman accepts the war she went through and is ennobled be her scars."~Carly Simon

L ife takes two directions to testing a person's will. Either it's nothing happening at all or everything happening at all or everything happening at once. Either way, a person of true strength knows that whichever direction life takes you it won't define you or destroy you. When I lost my son, I decided to pick up the pieces and continue to be a mother to my other children. I refused to let his death destroy me by living in fear for my son and daughter for the rest of our lives.

When I lost my home, the experience taught me to be more responsible with money. When I decided to love myself after many failed attempts getting others to love me, I discovered that was really all I needed to be truly happy and at peace. The recent and not so recent events of my life all have one thing in common. They are all responsible for helping me to evolve into a stronger woman.

My personal evolution is still a progress, and I'm learning more that whatever I reflect in the universe, the universe will give back to me tenfold. As I've mentioned earlier. If I want love, consistency, and respect, I have to give all of those to myself first. The love, consistency, and respect from others will follow. Once the universe sees that I'm giving myself what I need, success and money will come, because I remained persistent and committed to my passion. It's really just that simple.

This all proves that life isn't hard to live. We as people can make it complicated if we allow it to be. Of course, we all have to be mindful of outside forces like toxic people or unexpected circumstances that don't compliment our journeys. They make their way into our lives and cause distress, but that is when we'll use our best judgment. It's all a part of living your best life to the fullest, even through trials and tribulations.

Life is teaching me to dance in the storm, because the sun will eventually come back out. I'm learning that my past challenges didn't define me as a failure or a woman who struggles. Instead, it has defined me as a woman of faith, courage, and triumph. Now, I'm honoring my soul with pride and the ability to accept what is, and what my life could be.

I'm not ashamed of the fact that it has taken me some time to get where I am emotionally and spiritually. What matters is that I'm recovering from the self-criticism, the self-inflicted emotional wounds, and the beliefs that snatched away my confidence piece by piece.

My next step is to learn patience, because good things require a lot of it, as well as time. Being impatient has caused me to make a lot of poor choices in my life. Therefore, practicing patience is needed to improve in the areas of my life that involves important decision making. I'm realizing that whatever isn't happening now doesn't mean it will never happen. With patience, comes the relief in knowing that taking the careful approach instead of an anxious one is always better.

The careful approach is better in order to achieve goals, plans, better relationships, or whatever desire you want to fulfill in your life. Patience allows things to fall into place. Patience is a sign of love and respect for self and others. It helps solves difficult problems that are sometimes hard to face. People who practice patience understand that situations have to unfold in their own time. Good things just don't happen, especially with impatient folks. I'm accepting patience as my key to everything I want in life. While I accept patience, my intent is to work harder to achieve everything I want in my life.

Chapter 16

"I'm not kissing a damn frog to get my Prince

Charming!" Lakia Nichole

Y ou've probably read the quote, and is thinking that I'm crazy! Rest assured, I mean exactly that, except the part about the frog. I'm just trying to be funny, but seriously, I wonder about all the fairy tales that were read to us as little girls. The cartoons where the princess and her prince lives happily ever-after and the movies that glorified romance in such a beautiful way. It made me feel as though love was perfect, and the source of all of our happiness, until I grew up and realized that love is anything but what is perceived. I wondered why my mom never told me how hard it would be.

Sometimes, I want to call her and say, "Ma, what's up with that?" In all honesty, our moms can give us but so much advice on how to love a man, and maintain a great relationship, but it is ultimately up to us as women on how we do it. We can fall in love with a great man, a man who is not so great, or we can just fall in love with the idea of being in love, and not seeing the man beyond his exterior. I must admit that I was one of those women who couldn't tell the difference.

Love takes a lot of hard work to build and even more of hard work to stay in it! Love is not what is pretended to be in movies, television, and in Disney cartoons, where they pretty much confuse our little girls, as we speak! We used to suck our teeth and shake our heads at the sappy love music when it came on the radio, until we've experienced what the singer is talking about. That's when we stand and praise to it like we're in church catching the Holy Ghost!

I think EVERY man should fall in love with me! I'm not vain or conceited, but for every other woman who thinks the same way, I'm pretty sure y'all understand. So, why is the dating scene so damn hard for a lot of us? It's the "Prince charming" mentality that has really fucked up our heads! Our expectations of romance and falling in love are high, believing it could be a beautiful thing to experience all the time, but in the REAL world, it takes a lot more than just getting the glass slipper.

The best love that you can have is the love that you can give yourself. I can love myself with all the love that is built inside of me to the core but honestly, there will come a time when I'll want to have someone that I love who will make me feel like I'm his world! I'm not going to spend my time searching for love. In searching for it, I feel I will come across nothing that will exude true love. Fairy Tales never taught us that love will come when it's ready and that could take a while.

Fairy Tales never taught us about the downside of love as well. I believe that we as parents should teach our kids that it's not all peaches and cream, and we need to tell them about the non- Fairy Tale version of love and being patient with it. The reality of love between a man and a woman is that it has to be felt and built from the ground up from both. Make sure you're in love with the person, and not the idea of being in love.

Sometimes, people can't even tell when love exists, because they're blind to it. Love can smack them in the face, but to them it's assault. Love is basically what you put into it. Either you

put your all into love, or it will break you down.
No movie, cartoon, and even music can tell you
that much.

As a single woman, I've known for quite
some time that the word "LOVE" can be used
many ways. The definition itself has been
changed quite a few times by people who don't
really know how to love. I searched for love, and
tried to create it with men who were only
looking for just a "friendship with benefits". I
didn't pay attention to what was, because my
heart was telling my mind that each man I
became involved with would eventually be my
man with time. I was doing "girlfriend things"
and being faithful, when they were clearly not
my "boyfriend", and was far from faithful

themselves. I put my heart on the line, one man after another.

The more hurt I got from each situation, the more I deprived myself from accepting real love. After repeated disappointments, I didn't want anything to do with men. I became bitter and thought love sucked. I was clueless to know what true love could really do for me if I would've learned to love myself first. I've realized that once I stop searching for love, work on rebuilding self-love from the inside out, and focus more on important things in my life, I can take the focus off the need for love from a man. I've learned that I can't rush love and when it hits you, it will hit you like a ton of bricks.

My heart, mind and my body is way too precious to just share with just any man. He has to prove to me that his heart, mind, and body are just as worthy. I'm not perfect but if he can see past my faults, he will definitely deserve my best. Being in love can be a great feeling, but I believe what makes it work is when you love yourself more, and not accept anything less than loyalty and respect from the person you adore. I am proud of the fact that I no longer feel the need to be loved by a man to feel whole or complete. If I knew then what I know now.....................

Chapter 17

"Single... It's not just a status. It's actually a word that best describes a person who is strong enough to live and enjoy life without having to depend on others."~Unknown

I love being a single woman. It doesn't mean I want to stay single forever. However, this free time gives me the opportunity for personal growth. I'm also at a critical point in my life where I need to be selfish with time. If I'm not spending quality time with my children, I'm utilizing time to improve Lakia, to embrace Lakia, to have fun with Lakia, and love Lakia.

I believe the only disadvantage to not having a "boo" is going to bed alone at night, but the advantages outweighs the disadvantages by a ton. I don't think about going to bed alone. I have the rest of my life (God willing) to meet a man who is worthy of sharing my bed with.

Right now, I really appreciate the benefits of being single. I have no one to answer to and to be honest, I like the idea of having "options". When I hear the term "think like a man", I understand the true meaning behind it. Generally, men aren't consumed with the idea of long term relationships when it comes to meeting a lady. They'll go on dates ideally for the fun of it, while a lot of us women date with the purpose of finding a husband. There's nothing wrong with that if the man you're seeing is seeking a wife.

Unfortunately, shit happens within relationships, and it's not fair for him or for you to put that kind of pressure on yourself. I've applied that type of pressure to myself for years and trust me it doesn't make dating fun at all. Thinking like a man when it comes to dating takes a lot of pressure off of finding "the one" and just enjoying the company you're entertaining.

Being a single woman allows me to be more observant, and I find myself listening to men with a clearer ear and a clearer mind when getting to know them. I used to be so consumed with wanting a relationship that I only heard what I wanted to hear when a man told me he cared for me, and enjoyed my company....BUT. There was always that signature word "BUT" that told me I was what they wanted but not what they needed. I chose to have selective hearing with anything after the word "but". Now that I'm not consumed with wanting a relationship, I accept a man for who he is and what he wants. That leads to a better understanding of how to invest in the relationship.

Being a single woman has helped me find the woman I was meant to be. Being single has taught that I don't have to depend on a man to have fun with life. Being single gave me the opportunity to become emotionally empowered. Being single is making me wiser, as I refuse to end up in a relationship and still feel alone. Since I've embraced singlehood, I see things a lot more clearly. I understand that being single doesn't mean you're lonely, just like being in a relationship doesn't always make you happy. That's another reason for me to believe that I don't need to be with a man to be happy. Happiness truly comes from within. Happiness is accepting all that is happening in your life with flaws and all.

Being a single woman has given me time to adjust to the changes that has occurred within me. I used to be afraid of being single, until I got tired of throwing myself into something that felt remotely close to a relationship with a man, only to lose my identity, as a result. It has helped me re-discover my identity and the woman you see today is a confident vibrant woman who is not crying over the men who chose other women over her like she used to. In fact, I congratulate them, because they are who they're supposed to be with.

When the man God blesses me with enters my life, I'll be grateful. Until then, I'm appreciating the gift of time that God is blessing me with. Being single is currently the best thing that is happening to me. My status has helped me to discover myself, in turn helps me to decide what I want in a partner. It has helped me to discover what I truly like, dislike, and what makes me tick when it comes to romance. Since being single, I'm able to dedicate more time to my writing career. Hence, the reason you're reading this book. Overall, I can make my life any way I want it to be without limitations or pressure from a partner. I look forward to sharing my life with the man of my dreams. However, he'll have to respect the fact that I had dreams and goals before I met him, and I don't intend to change or ignore them because we're in a relationship. That's it and that's all!

Living single is a lot easier when you take the pressure off of committing to someone. I've gained the "letting the chips fall where they may" type of mentality. I have no more room in my life for self-pity and loneliness. Those days are long gone, and with wonderful friends, a fulfilling social life, and very active children, why would not having a man make me feel lonely?

The stereotype of single women disturbs me, though. Society's perception of us is that we're either promiscuous or crazy is absurd, as well as a double standard. Single men will be perceived as a stud in a heartbeat. As much as I cannot stand the questions I get sometimes which are "Why aren't you married yet?" and

"Why are you still single?" I answer honestly that it's simply not my time.

Singleness is not a disease that you catch on the street. It's a way of life and in some cases, the direction that should be taken. Personally, it's saving me from personal and emotional destruction. I've suffered enough in half-ass relationships to know that society doesn't determine when I should be in a relationship, I do. I'm single by choice and will remain so, until otherwise.

Chapter 18

"Success consists of going from failure to failure

without loss of enthusiam." Winston

Churchill

I'm sure every other writer have thought of this; selling over a million books, sitting on Oprah's or Ellen's couch, getting invited to the hottest literary and red carpet events, and living the ultimate luxurious lifestyle. It all sounds familiar, right? Well, that was my dream when I published my first novel. I was going to become famous with my book. I was going to sell so many copies that Tyler Perry's people was going to call me in regards to turning it into a feature film. I was going to be the "Beyonce'" of the literary industry, except I didn't work hard enough to achieve that amount of success. I chose to slack in certain areas of promotion, thinking I didn't have to work too hard to become noticeable in the literary game.

Well, I've certainly fooled myself and as a result, my dream of sitting on Oprah's couch never happened. I was lazy and lacked enthusiasm when I realized book promotion required a lot more than posting Facebook updates. I lost my passion for writing when I became disappointed in my sales. I blamed people privately for not being avid book readers, when in fact it had nothing to do with them. My excuse publicly was taking on other projects, which was partly true. My actions created my results. However, I'm still proud of the fact that I've accomplished my goal to become a published author. I've learned that money and fame should not have been my primary focus. Focusing on the fame actually took away the focus from the promotion.

Today, I take my career as an author a lot more seriously. I'm not so focused on sitting on Oprah and Ellen's couch although that would be nice. My focus is promotion, promotion, and promotion. Every interview, book signing, and book club meeting matters, and it's my responsibility to book them if I want to spread the word about my publishing company. Hard work is definitely the key to success, and trust me...I've been working my ass off.

After the failed attempts to making television appearances, and movie deals with Tyler, I decided that my desires should be manifested with a more realistic mindset. Today, my capacity for hard work has improved while still reaching for success, which I know I can still achieve. At one point, I was afraid of my potential because of where I could possibly end up if I became unstoppable. It doesn't make sense, but it does. Have you ever had that overwhelming feeling that you could actually be beyond successful at what you love to do? Have you ever felt intimidated by the thought? Well, that actually held me back for some time, until I decided to stop being a punk. What made me stop being a punk? It's the belief that I could reach the top and not fall. It is knowing that opportunities are endless if I step out of my own way. It is wanting to dive into the pool of success and feel how refreshing I know it can be.

I understand now that there is enough room for me to achieve success like everyone else, and I shouldn't be afraid of it. I shouldn't be afraid of anything that's welcoming. Success is calling my name, and I hear it loud and clear. I hear the echoes of my name being called every time I put forth effort. I understand that even though I haven't taken a seat on Oprah's couch, I still achieved some amounts of success by doing exactly what I said I was going to do. I said I wanted to have my own publishing company, and with persistence and dedication, I have one. It's proof that if I can dream it, I can achieve it. It's up to me to do the work for me to achieve.

Chapter 19

You are imperfect, permanently and inevitably

flawed, and you are beautiful." Amy Bloom

I'm learning to love my body, despite the significant pooch that protrudes from my mid-section. I believe all women and even some men are struggling with one body part while embracing another body part. I've been fighting my belly fat for years and during intimacy, it's hard to concentrate on the act because I'm too worried about what he'll think once he sees my belly. I've had conversations with men who say that they don't care about that. If they've gone as far as share intimacy with you, then they obviously have some attraction to you.

Unfortunately, it's a burden on my self-esteem, as well as shopping for apparel. My pooch has kept me from purchasing a few cute dresses and tops, and I want to get to a point where I don't have to rely on a girdle. Now, I'm working to get a Janet Jackson belly. It's not easy, especially for a food addict such as myself. I'll eat healthy for a whole week then next week, I'll fall off the wagon by devouring some egg foo yung. It's so unfair that I can't eat everything I want!

The good thing is I've been a lot more active than I've been in years.

With at-home yoga, dance class, my fast-paced job position, and an occasional girls night out to shake my ass, my body gets a good enough workout. I am trying, and I think it's safe to say that I'm no quitter. When I get intimate with a man, I want to anticipate taking off my top, because my abs look like you can bounce a quarter on them. I can say that I've been watching what I eat for months, but I still have work to do. A six pack abs is my goal, but if my energy can only get me two packs, I'll be just as satisfied. Now that I've shared with you the body part that I struggle with, let me share with you the body part that I love....MY ASS.

My ass came from out of nowhere when I was in grade school. At first, I was embarrassed about my plump behind. I loathed the attention I got from the little boys in my class. It made me very uncomfortable because as a fifth grader, I didn't know how to accept the fact that I was blossoming. Not only did I have a butt, but my hips were starting to form, and so were my breasts.

When I was a high schooler, I purposely wore clothes a couple of sizes too big as often as I could to cover my curves. Some of my peers thought I was a tomboy. It wasn't until I reached my late teens when I began to embrace my curves, including my rear end. As the days passed, so did my need to dress in big attire. I packed away all of the big sized clothes, and started dressing more feminine. I even began to walk differently, because I felt like a woman. Embracing my curves even help me accept the attention I received from my male peers. I no longer felt embarrassed, but more confident.

I love having an ass. However, I don't want to be known for it. I understand that my male peers may have a hard time looking past a female with a nice ass, but for me I'd love to receive attention for something else like my sense of humor. That would make me feel even sexier, and he would get major points.

From Jennifer Lopez to Kim Kardashian, it seems like having an ass is all the rave. Unfortunately, some women have resorted to injections, which is super dangerous and very unnecessary in my opinion but to each her own. I want to thank my mama for giving me my ass naturally. Until I lose the tummy fat, I'll have to resort to some gut-squeezing apparatus, but my ass will look great in that mini dress.

184 | P a g e

Chapter 20

"It is not sex that gives the pleasure, but the lover."~ Marge Piercy

I consider myself to be very sexual. I love sex in many different forms, different ways, and different positions. It's an indescribable feeling when it's with a person you've yearned for, and care about. One of my many missions in life is to find a lover who matches my sexual prowess. One who knows how to take his time with exploring every inch of my body from my hair follicles to my toenails with his hands and tongue.

It takes a very special man of dexterity with his body to take me to that special place intimately without basic sexual moves. You know what I mean...the ones who think humping like a porn star is going to do the trick. Nothing wrong with sex like that, because the force from hardcore sexual intercourse is what personally gets me going when I'm in the mood for it.

However, I need variation with more delicate sex. Someone that's delicate with his hands, finger tips, and lips that'll arouse all of my senses with every touch. I think it's important for anyone involved in a sexual relationship to keep the communication going. If there's anything that he/she is lacking in that area, don't be afraid to speak about it.

As humans, we deserve sexual pleasure, and if you're not sexually satisfied with your partner, be honest and tell him/her, so that the both of you can come to a solution where you both can stay satisfied. I've had two partners who didn't fully satisfy me, but I never opened up about what they lacked in for fear of hurting the ego, or worse--the relationship. One was great with being spontaneous, but his penis was small. A couple of years later, I became involved with the other who was the complete opposite, having a great-sized penis, but lacked creativity.

I looked past the sexual shortcomings of them both because I cared for them. It was frustrating to say the least, but I didn't want to lose them. It was proof that I was prepared to be sexually unsatisfied for the rest of my life, as long as I was in a relationship. My mind was distorted with the belief that I didn't need or deserved to be fulfilled sexually. I was getting sex regularly and that was all that mattered to me at the time. I didn't understand that the man I was giving my body to was getting all he needed, while I still yearned for more after he was done.

It's like I was feeding him a steak and potatoes meal, while he was feeding me cereal. I was still hungry afterwards. It was such an unfair exchange, but I dealt with it. I felt it was enough, because of who he was. Both relationships eventually ended for other reasons, but they've taught me the importance of communicating with those you exchange sexual energy with. If you're not satisfied after it's over, you're defeating the purpose of performing the intimate act. As I've mentioned earlier, I am practicing celibacy. I know what you're thinking; how can someone who loves sex practice celibacy?

It's simple...Just because I'm waiting to have sex, it doesn't mean I can't appreciate one of the most naturally human acts of mankind. Besides, my celibacy coexists with my desires to experience a more passionate and intimate form of love. My celibacy is not about saving sex for marriage, although I'm not against it. While practicing, I'm learning to be generally honest and open with men. In turn, being capable of opening up about what I like sexually with a man I'm dating, should I choose to become intimate with him.

Chapter 21

"Your lost self esteem may take longer to find than a new boyfriend, so prioritize accordingly."~Unknown

F rom my late teens to my mid thirties, I've suffered from low self esteem. When you're a person who looks to men to validate your fierceness which I used to do, you are struggling with low self esteem. When you compare your beauty to the beauty of other women which I used to do, you're struggling with low self esteem. I never knew how severe my low self esteem was until I reached my late thirties. Every phone call, text, email, touch, hug, kiss, and intercourse from my guy mattered so much, because they all made me feel special. Special in a way that all the forms of communication and intimacy made me feel better as a woman.

I was a woman who felt cared for and loved, not knowing that I didn't need love and care from a man to make me feel better or complete. One guy I dated was someone who I was sure was "the one", and he made me feel like a princess. Out of all of the men, he was the only one who has done romantic things like surprise me by bringing flowers to my job, and surprised me with candlelight dinners. He was that guy who I assumed loved me, because I was never treated like that before. The flowers and candlelight dinners was all new to me. He never told me that he loved me, but that's what the special treatment felt like. My friends and I used to joke that a guy could change my light-bulb, and we'd fall in love. I was so impressed with the dinner that night that I couldn't wait to tell my friends the next day.

Being familiar with my history with men, because I tell my friends almost everything regarding the men I date, their reaction after I told them about my candlelit dinner was not what I expected. They were happy for me, until I told them that I gave him some. They immediately criticized me for giving it up too soon. They thought it would have been smarter for me to make him wait. They said that a candlelit dinner wasn't something that he deserved sex for. I thought they were jealous, because I had a "boo" who was romantic. They were all right and I was being a love-sick dummy. I didn't realize how fast I moved, until later that night.

My conversation with my girls kept me up most of the night. Deep down, I knew they had my best interest at heart, and like I mentioned earlier. They gave me criticism filled with love. It was criticism that I needed in order to stop thinking with my vagina and start thinking with a mind full of sense. I eventually stopped seeing him, because I wanted more time with him and he couldn't provide the time that I needed. His excuse was because he worked a lot but looking back, I believe I got too clingy for him.

The last few texts to him, I accused him of seeing other women. I showed true possession on my part and that wasn't good. We were only dating for a month after we both agreed to take our friendship to the next level. The break up with this particular guy hurt me more than the others, because we grew up together. We were childhood friends who grew to become adults and became attracted to one another. When I thought we were getting closer, we were actually breaking apart.

Once I realized it was over, my esteem weakened more. I needed love because I felt more alive with it. Besides, who else was going to buy me flowers and cook me dinner without me having to ask? I wanted him to be with me, because I felt secure giving my love to this man who treated me like no other. My fragile heart felt like they were in good hands with this man, because of the extra steps he's taken to make me feel special.

After we stopped seeing each other, I went into a depression. I couldn't deal with the reality that I wasn't with the man who I thought had fallen in love with me. I suffered from serious writer's block as a result, and that hindered my writing career. I struggled with a combination of low self esteem and relationship addiction, in which both was detrimental to my soul.

When I finally regained the strength to lift myself from the depression, I picked up the pieces to my broken heart and glued it back together with my own love. I had enough of feeling down, and if I wanted nice flowers I was going to buy them myself. I took my mind to a place before that guy and I reconnected. I pretended that what happened between us never happened for me to move on with life. I tried to erase the memories that we've created, by burying myself into my writings.

I've learned that I don't need a man to make me feel whole, complete, or even loved. If I knew then what I knew now, the time I used being depressed would've been invested in celebrating the rejection, because it was truly a blessing. That relationship taught me what I could do for myself to feel special.

It taught me that I'm all woman. I am at my very best without a man. I am enough, and a man who sees me as such will be the one who deserves my body. It will also take more than dinner and flowers to prove that. I'm learning that if a man plans to stick around with me flaws and all, he will say so without manipulation with gifts that he knows I'm not accustomed to receiving.

Maybe he romanced me with genuine interest in me or maybe he didn't. I'll never know and honestly, I don't care to know. What matters is the lesson I've learned; To stop moving too fast, to stop giving myself the short end of the stick when dealing with men, and know that I am enough of a woman without a man in my life.

Chapter 22

"The life of the dead is placed in the memory of the living."~ Marcus Tullius Cicero

W hen my son died, I felt compelled to express my thoughts in form of written words a few days later, so I wrote this poem/letter that I wanted to share.

I don't question God

But I had to ask why?

Why my baby boy?

so young, so sweet, too soon

Then God said to me...

"Robert was a precious gift to you and your family

He was here to fulfill a purpose. And now that his purpose was fulfilled

I must return him back to me."

Then I asked

He had so many years to live!

Then God said to me...

"It doesn't matter how many years he lived on earth.

It's the lives he touched while he was here that matters

Robert has succeeded the journey of an angel.

Don't ever worry, for Robert is in good hands."

God had lifted me up off my knees and wiped my tears

I'm accepting the fact that my baby boy is gone.

It's not easy....

nor will it ever be

But, now I have my own personal angel to look after me.

When I see my kids watch cartoons together, I will see your spirit sitting next to them

When I listen to my son play with his cars, I will also hear your voice when he goes "vroom vroom"

When I lay down at night, I will always feel your little body lie next to mine

Every time I close my eyes, I will feel your tiny arms wrapped around me & hear those four little words
in my ear say "Mommy, I love you"

I'm gonna miss you so much and I need you here with me

But now I understand that God need you more.

Your job here is done

I miss you & I love you baby

Your Mommy,
Lakia

I understand now that Heaven couldn't wait for Robert. Like special gifts, the presence of my son was so special, that his life was only to last a few short years. I sometimes wonder if God sent him home early because he has foreseen the evils of the world that would taint his innocence as an older child. It was one of the few theories that I could come up with as to why my son was taken. I stopped focusing so much on why and how, because I didn't want to get to a place emotionally and become stuck there.

Accepting Robert's death was something I never thought I could do, until I made the choice to keep living the life that I was given. I also have two other children that need me. They also needed to witness an example of not letting life's obstacles keep you down. I had to accept his death, not only for myself but for them.

You know what keeps me smiling when I think of him? It's the memories and picturing what heaven is like with him there. I sometimes wonder if transitioned people's spirits age like we do in body form. Would Robert, as well as my father (who he's named after) be the same age when we finally reunite? I even wonder about reincarnation. I look around at random people, including folks I don't know and wonder if our loved ones are reborn into someone else, living a different life.

I wonder if God gives spirits a chance at starting over physically with life differently from the last life they were given, or do spirits simply float around in heaven. Or is it both? I have so many questions about heaven. I know, however, that Robert has made it there and is not alone and that makes me accept his death a lot easier. Today, if a random person asks me how many children I have, I say one girl and one son. I sometimes feel like I discredit Robert's memory by leaving him out, but I don't want the reactions I get. I'm not looking for pity parties.

I'll never fully heal from Robert's death, but I can still get to my happy place with memories of him that I'll cherish forever. I even have a "memory box" with his favorite things that I like to look through every now and then. Memories are mental photographs that will never fade. I have memories of him from his birth to his last days that will forever keep a smile on my face.

Chapter 23

"A rejection is nothing more than a necessary step in the pursuit of success."~ Bo Bennett

Rejection can put a huge hole in your confidence and self-esteem, especially when it's from the opposite sex. I can't even count on my fingers the many times I've been rejected, and it's really a hard pill to swallow to not be accepted by someone you're interested in or care about. I've lost a little of my confidence with every "no", every ignored call or text, every avoidance, and every blow to the heart after sexual intercourse. I questioned my ability to live up to their standards, and yes living by my own standards wasn't quite important.

Instead of wanting to be the woman I was meant to be, my goal was to become the woman that I thought they would want to be with. At the same time, I was losing my identity. I was also a confused mess with the men I've dealt with. If they didn't want me as myself, or as a woman with traits and characteristics they admired, then who do they want? I began to question if I was even capable of being in a relationship. I felt totally unwanted and undesirable. Then I got some sense.....

I finally got tired of trying to prove to men that I was right for them. When I began to love myself more, I came to an understanding that rejection is simply a sign that the person isn't capable of loving like you do. In fact, he is giving you the freedom to find someone who does.

All of those rejections I've encountered are seen as blessings. I didn't see that then, because my mind was clouded with ways to improve for him. I was fine the way I was the whole time and I didn't realize that. I was totally wanted and desirable, and my beauty that I carried internally just wasn't meant for any of them to see. I believe that worrying about being rejected is helpful when dating someone new. Although, we all like to make good impressions, it's also healthier not to focus on the "what ifs" when it comes to dating. I'm learning to just enjoy dating when it happens.

Rejection is one of those disguised blessings. When you think something bad is happening, it's actually a step to something greater.

After my many experiences with rejection, I've learned not to go chasing after someone who has already rejected me. The rejection has happened for a good reason and besides, I shouldn't be doing the chasing anyway. I believe women aren't supposed to do the chasing, because we're the choosers. This leads me to the question when it comes to approaching men.

Do we approach men we're interested in or not? I've approached men before and discovered that when I've done so, I set the parameters for the relationship. It didn't stop with approaching the man, it continued with asking him out, and doing other random things that society says a man should do for the woman. He basically got accustomed to me initiating everything. There's nothing wrong with that if that's what you don't mind doing. However, if you want consistency and not feel like the one who has to initiate everything, then give him the chance to make the first moves. I mentioned earlier that women should think like men when it comes to dating, but that's from an emotional standpoint.

By dating standards, I believe women should allow men to make the first move. I think approaching men overall is a win/lose situation, but the end of the day you do what you feel is right. Personally, I've had enough of making the first move. I need something different. I need to feel like a man is interested in me enough to ask me out. I haven't figured that out yet because during most of my encounters with men, it was I who came up with most ideas and plans to get together. This is why patience is important and necessary for me.

The next time I get into a position of dating, I need to practice patience to see where it'll take me. Instead of jumping up and asking him to go out, I need to see if he has enough interest in me to ask me out. If he does, that's great. If he's doesn't, that's great too. It proves that he's not that into me, and you know what? I'll still be my fierce and fantastic self.

Chapter 24

"Ride the energy of your own unique spirit."~

Gabrielle Roth

I'm five feet, one inch tall at currently one-hundred and fifty pounds, so I'm not "modelesque", and I'm okay with that. I consider myself friendly to everyone, but it takes a while to open up to new people, and I'm okay with that. I'm not too reserved, but I'm not out of control. I'm that perfect balance of being adventurous, and I'm okay with that. Trying on jeans at the store can be a challenge, because my thighs do what they want to do, but I'm okay with that.

The perfect Friday night consists of Netflix and my favorite wine over any night club or lounge, and I'm okay with that. Not every guy will think I'm beautiful. In fact, some may think I'm unattractive, and I'm okay with that. I'm not here to please everyone except myself, and that special someone who wants my love. I'm embracing my faults and flaws, and my overall uniqueness.

I have one eye slightly bigger than the other, and I love it. I procrastinate at times, but that's okay. While I procrastinate, I take the time to make sense of things, and weigh the pros and cons before I make major decisions. I've learned that embracing who I am is the greatest form of self- love, and I don't need to change for anyone. Changing yourself for the pursuit of others to accept you can be emotionally and spiritually draining. I refuse to no longer invest time with people that cannot accept me for who I am.

Who am I? I am a woman of substance; character, backbone, prosperity, courage, peace, style, significance, and class. It's taken a long time to discover my uniqueness and embrace it fully. It's taken me a long time to understand that being rejected had nothing to do with who I am. The steps I've taken to accept myself were during a critical time when I was at my lowest. I was tired of feeling like I had nothing to offer to the world.

I started with setting an intention for myself by shifting paradigms. I stopped the pattern of self-loathing in order to live a more satisfying life. I deserve a life without fear, doubt, and shame. I began a new pattern in which I became less critical of myself. I also decided to celebrate my strengths.

As humans who strive for perfection, we can't help but point out flaws and shortcomings before anything else. I had to remind myself that perfection is simply an illusion. I take a look back at all the hardships I overcame and all of the goals I've accomplished thus far. My strength helped me get to where I am.

Without strength, I would have quit many times in my life. The next two steps were the most critical and most important out of all of them in helping me accept myself for who I am, and that was forgiving myself and silencing my inner critic. Forgiving was major for me, because in order for me to accept myself I had to forgive the regrets from my past struggles with everything. I accepted the fact that I can't and couldn't change the past, and I'm making continuous efforts to grow and learn. I told my inner critic to shut the hell up and I haven't heard from her since. If I make a mistake from this moment on, I'll learn from it. It will not make me any less of a good woman, smart woman, or a confident woman.

One thing in particular about myself that I can appreciate more than anything right now is my ability to fall in love kind of fast. I know you've read that and think that is how I ended up struggling with the men in my past. While that may be true, wearing my heart on my sleeve is not a flaw or a fault of mine. There's a guy out there who loves just like I do. God is simply working on him, while he's working on me.

Chapter 25

"Sex is like pizza. When it's good, it's good. When it's bad, it's still pretty good."Unknown

Ever think about someone and say "I wish I could UNfuck this person!"? It's the experience you've had where you were put into a vulnerable position with someone who clearly wasn't worthy of you. Not because the sex was bad, but the person was just not the right person for you. For me, it was all about the confusion I had with distinguishing the difference between needing dick and wanting dick. Back then, I thought I needed dick when in fact I just wanted it, no matter the emotional detachment of the man. I was DICKmatized as I've mentioned earlier, or what some folks say DICKstracted.

When we need dick, we haven't had it in a while and when the opportunity presents itself to get it, we'll take it. When we just want dick, we'll just be ready to give up the vagina at any time, even though we've just had some two nights ago. In both situations, the man can either have genuine feelings for us or just want the vagina with no strings attached.

The problem with that is in most cases, we as women don't know the intentions until afterwards. When we find out that he isn't that into us, or worse avoids us after sexual intercourse we become emotionally distraught, because we wanted something more with him. None of that would have happened if we didn't become dickmatized or dickstracted.

I understand now that taking time with men is beneficial in so many ways. I've rushed intimacy with men, because I felt like I had to snatch them up quick for them to stay interested in me. I used sex as a means to get and keep their attention. I didn't understand the fact that all I had to do was remain my charming self to keep a man's attention.

I made so many mistakes in my past, but giving it up too soon was a wakeup call for me to change my impatient ways. I'm not dating anyone currently by choice and by force. My current living situation forces me not to date but honestly, not dating is doing me some good. Not dating is helping me to focus more on my writing career. I'm also using this free time to build up will power, self control, and self-encouragement.

I sometimes wonder what could happen when I start to date again. Will I become dickstracted too soon or will my desire to be greater than I once was take in effect? Well, I'm striving to have the relationship that I deserve. That could only mean that history will not repeat itself. I'd like to see where waiting goes. Waiting will show a guy's true intentions for me. Waiting will empower my ability to stand firm in my beliefs that I am worthy of a solid genuine loving relationship.

When you've gone through enough bullshit, you'll get tired enough to want change. They say if you want different results, you have to stop doing the same things. I'm taking a different direction with men to get better results, and I believe it will pay off. I want to thank each man I became involved with, because my experiences with them all have taught me a valuable lesson. I forgive them for the hurt they've caused.

I also forgive myself for allowing the hurt, but I definitely thank them. They've taught me what to look out for, what I need, what I don't deserve, and what I'm worthy of. If I had the option to do it all over again I wouldn't change a thing. I'm a lot smarter now than a couple of years ago. Each man is responsible for how I treat myself today. I'm going to apply what I've learned towards the next potential relationship. I owe it to my mind, body, and soul to be more patient, attentive, and cautious with men I'm attracted to.

A letter to my ten year old self

*D*ear Lakia (10 yrs old),

As an adult of you now, I must write this letter & let you know that you have grown up to be a respectable, down to earth & sweet adult. You were a shy little girl, a little bit on the "tom boy" side, but as you grew, you've embraced your femininity. Much like now, you were constantly thinking of ways to have fun when boredom struck. Now, as an adult...you work hard to improve the quality of your life (while you remain a kid at heart). Back then, you wanted to be different things (a teacher, a lawyer, a dancer, an actress) but with all the writing you were doing, the adult in you never would've realized that you can turn it into a business & something you enjoy doing. I admire your determination to do what you've always wanted to do...& that was to simply write.

Of course, I bet you'd never expect to go through what you've been through in 2011. I'm so sorry you had to lose many loved ones, including your child. But the adult in you have strength beyond measure. You were able to move on & continue to live life, even though part of you died with your son. Prayer & your support system definitely helped you.

You are a very strong adult now, & as you continue to become challenged romantically, financially, & professionally...I know things will turn around eventually with continued strength, prayer, not giving up on your dream, & seeing the beautiful things that life can offer.
I am extremely proud of the adult you have grown to become.

Love,
Lakia (the adult)

Chapter 26

"Time is what we want most, but what we use worst."~ William Penn

Time is the most precious gift which we sometimes take for granted. Time gives us the chance to start over, to think things through. Time gives us the chance to make the right choices, and to accomplish something. Once you spend time, you cannot get it back. I've spent a lot of time making numerous mistakes, but I've also spent time making up for them.

Time allows you to grow, conquer, plan, learn, and basically everything you do in order to evolve. Don't waste time looking back, repeating the same thing expecting different results, or doing absolutely nothing while believing success is just going to fall in your lap.

I love having time to enjoy what life offers, and I look forward to every joyous moment that comes my way. I try to revel in time, because time goes by quickly. Before you'll know it, the present is the past, and the future is the present. Managing your time is very important, and with time management come prioritization.

As a single mother getting her business off the ground, it was necessary for me to split my time up into four categories. This would help prevent me from becoming overwhelmed with life's daily routines. My four categories are Relaxing, Building, Socializing, and Me time.

- **Relaxing:** Isn't it obvious? After work, I go straight to writing, while attending to the kids and preparing them for the next day. Taking the time to relax helps me recharge. If I don't take time to relax, WATCH OUT!

- **Building:** I also utilize time working on my business. When I'm not writing, I'm networking with other literary associates, promoting, marketing, and strategizing.

- **Socializing:** When the kids are away (or with their dad, or a sitter) the adults will play. I need to socialize. As a "public figure" it's pretty necessary if I want to be well-known for what I do. I enjoy spending a night out with my girlfriends, as well. When you let loose, let your hair down, and paint the town red with your friends, it brings you a certain sense of joy. Having fun keeps you young at heart. Getting out, even if it's just once in awhile matters. Especially if you're a parent.

- **Me time:** The purpose for having "me time" runs along the same as relaxing. Except, there's no one around. It's just you and your peace of mind. Having time for yourself is mandatory, in my opinion. It helps maintain your sanity, and keeps you from going bald from pulling hairs.

Do what you enjoy during me time. Go to a movie, do some yoga, listen to music, read, or just relax in a quiet setting with only the sound of your breathing.

Time well spent helps me discover the fundamentals of a good life. I know that whatever I seek in life that brings me happiness, joy, peace, and stability I'll find with time. Every good thing in life takes time to manifest, so I'm learning not to rush.

Trust me when I say, rushing doesn't get us anywhere but to a dead end or worse--crash. I'm taking my time with all aspects of my life, so that I can maneuver around the blocks and obstacles that I'm prepared to face. Only then will I make it through my journey without missing what's important.

Chapter 27

"Music was my refuge. I could crawl into the space between the notes and curl my back to loneliness."~Maya Angelou

There was a period in my life when I went through loneliness and hopelessness. I didn't stay in touch with my extended family, I had no boyfriend, and I had a falling out with a close friend. Feeling hopeless stemmed from my literary career not going anywhere. I also had to move back home with my mother, because I lost the house I shared with my cousin. The only thing that was supplying peace and keeping me from becoming depressed about everything was music.

After a typical day of working and tending to the kids, my night always ended up listening to music that made me feel good. I will not name the group, but their music in particular leaves me with amazing memories, as well as amazing fantasies. Those who know me personally know of the group of which I speak about. However, due to the nature of this chapter, the group's name will be intentionally left out.

Their music took my mind off my troubles, and my inability to exist outside of my own little personal world. I've been a fan of this particular group for many years, and while I came to admire other groups who have come and gone, it is THIS particular group's music that's always affected me personally.

Because of the wonderful age of technology and social media, I (and other fans) was able to connect with one of the group's members on Twitter and oddly enough, he was my "favorite" of the group. I was also able to meet other fans of this group, which was also cool. The fans eventually became my new "extended family", and the group who we admired became "our boyfriends." This is where I began to struggle with loneliness.

Connecting with these people felt like one of the highlights of my life, because I felt like this group's music brought some amazingly cool people in my life. Because of our collective love for this group, a lot of fans had become my best buds, because I thought my true best buds didn't want anything to do with me during our fall out. I felt like this group's music brought people together, and at such a critical moment of my life. Because of my loneliness, I spent all of my extra time worshipping this group. Worshipping the group eventually turned into worshipping "my favorite" member. Things soon escalated as it became an obsession for this particular group member.

While listening to their music at night and instead of completing that book I was supposed to finish, I would take the time to find out anything and everything about my favorite group member. I would follow him on every social media site that he was on, so I could keep up with him. Instead of posting stuff about my book, I would repost just about everything he posted, in hopes I'd get his attention.

When I did get his attention, he made my day! When I didn't get his attention, I became disappointed. Oh! And anyone who talked bad about this group would've gotten a mouthful from me! For me, social media is all about networking with friends, family, and associates in your field. When I initially created a Twitter account, my purpose was to do just that. That is, until I found my celebrity crush. After months of just utilizing my Twitter to keep up with him, I lost followers. My obsession was so real, that I didn't even care. Half of the followers that still lingered didn't seem to care, because they shared my obsession.

After re-evaluating my behavior and doing some research, it's been concluded that I suffered from simple obsessional stalking. It defines an individual that has the inability to have successful personal relationships in their own lives, social awkwardness, feelings of powerlessness, a sense of insecurity, and very low self-esteem. Of these characteristics, low self-esteem plays a large role in the obsession that these individuals develop with their victim, in this case, the famous person.

If the individual is unable to have any sort of connection to the celebrity with which they are obsessed, their own sense of self-worth is said to decline or so they believe. That's why it was important for me to attend my first show to meet my favorite group, particularly my favorite group member. Not only because I wanted to attend their show for years, but if anything was going to go right at that time in my life, I was going to have a personal connection with my favorite group member. Why? He became my "boyfriend", taking the place of the one I needed in real life. I had to attend as many shows as I could. Why? Because hanging out with the fans was like being with friends and family, something I wasn't able to do with my real family and friends.

Looking back, I understand that my loneliness resulted in me needing to be a part of something special, so I looked to this group and their fan base exactly for that. Nothing else was going right in my life, and the only thing that brought me joy was their music and their interaction. I was in denial about my obsession, until I regained control of my life. I did that by gaining new and real friendships, rekindling old friendships, dating, and shifting my focus to what really mattered. I noticed the drastic change within myself in how I spent my free time. I was no longer cyber-stalking this man, chatting with other fans, and spending every free moment fantasizing about him.

Although, I still listen to their music, and still attend a show once in a while, I refuse to allow myself to get caught up in celebrity worshipping stuff when I have so much going for me now. Celebrity worshipping is irrelevant to my life now. There's nothing wrong with admiring your favorite star. However, I've learned that we should keep it about the entertainment. Anything more would require seeking what really makes you happy in your life.

Chapter 28

"Ladies, there's power in the pussy that some of you who have the pussy don't even know. It's ok to give away the pussy, but you should not give up its power."~ Author Al Saadiq Banks

In dedication to the quote above, I will repeatedly use the word pussy instead of vagina, because I feel like I'll be more convincing with my points of view with the word pussy. So, for those who are sensitive to the word, it's necessary. Sorry.

I've used my pussy for the wrong reasons many of times. The main reason was trying to manipulate the man into having something more with me, instead of just accepting what was. My pussy was basically used for enjoyment purposes by a man who didn't want to claim me as no more than a friend with benefits.

Each time I had sex, I was devaluing my pussy, not knowing because I was focused on just getting some. When I thought sex would bring me more respect and closeness, it had actually pushed me farther away. I got the game totally twisted and as a result, my pussy was losing its power. Sex was always easy to get, but that also meant love got harder for me to find. That's because I was using my pussy thinking it would give me the advantage of becoming committed.

Let's be clear about something. Material things like money, jewelry, shoes and stuff of that nature was never my intentions when giving away pussy. The guys I've dated weren't pulling coins like that, anyway. I've always used protection during sex. My intentions were love and attention, and because of my addiction to relationships I always felt the need for that closeness and that bond with a man. The deeper the intimacy, the closer I felt to being loved, even if I was never told "I love you". Do you remember the scene in *Harlem Nights* when "Sunshine" slept with that guy, then afterwards he called his wife and told her he was leaving her to be with Sunshine? Well, that's the mentality I carried about my pussy.

It was my belief that my pussy was going to change minds, and have the man fall totally in love with me. I've learned that there isn't that much great feeling pussy in the world that's going to make a man commit when he isn't ready. My pussy was powerful enough to get him to sleep with me, but it wasn't powerful enough to make him officially mine. It's taken many of pussy trials for me to grab that notion.

I think more logically and wiser with my pussy now. In turn, my pussy has regained some of it power, and it's also increasing in value. I told myself a long time ago that if I wanted a guy's love and attention, all I need to do is let him get to know me without the sex.

Exhibiting self love and respect will in turn show

him that is what I deserve. I don't need to use the

power from my pussy to make a man stay, and

truth be told if I have to make him stay and force

him to give me attention, he's not worth my time.

A man who is interested will do what's

necessary for him to spend time with you.

There's no need for sexual or emotional

manipulation. For me, the relationship addiction

is the source of why I use my pussy's power for

less than beneficial reasons. As I've said earlier,

it's my need to feel that closeness. I'm learning

that intimacy doesn't require giving away the

pussy.

The noun intimacy comes from the Latin word intimare, which means "impress," or "make familiar". That's something we can do simply with conversation. I can impress a man with not only my pussy, but I can impress him with my mind, as well. The key is to practice patience. With patience comes time. With time, comes a successful relationship. I'm learning. I'm a work in progress.

Chapter 29

"Never compare yourself to others, because God created you perfectly." Unknown

C omparing myself to other women was something else I used to do. It was during a period when I doubted my own beauty, wondering if I wasn't pretty enough to keep a guy's attention. This type of struggle lingered since my high school days when all the guys I had crushes on didn't like me, because they had crushes on my more "exotic" looking friends with baby hair or my light skinned friends.

As I entered adult hood my struggle continued, as I felt like sex was something that needed to happen to keep a guy's attention. For a while, my assumption was if an intellectual conversation and quality time out wasn't in the works, I might as well let him see what I'm working with. Maybe then he will start asking me out. Then I thought maybe I wasn't attractive enough for him to ask me out.

The negative thoughts about my beauty consumed me a great deal, and along with the relationship addiction that I had I wasn't allowing these men a chance to see my true worth. That's because I couldn't see my true worth. My mind was clouded with so much self-criticism and self-doubt, that any intimate act or kind word from a man that made me feel more beautiful or loved was acceptable, even if it was something as simple as a good morning text.

There were a couple of events where I discovered this guy spent so much time with one woman I knew. I became full with jealousy and green with envy for this woman who was taking up so much time with this guy. I began comparing my beauty to hers. This woman was strikingly pretty, locally well-known, and successful in her own right. Many of her attributes I strived for. I not only began comparing our beauty, but also our successes. I wasn't pretty like her, or popular, or everything else that she was. I started to believe I was a boring individual that men would not dare waste their time getting to know. I started to believe that all men that became involved with me only wanted me for sex.

They've all proved it the same way by stopping all forms of communication after getting as much vagina from me as they could. That is, until I got tired of the inconsistency. I developed the belief that I simply just wasn't enough for any man. I started telling myself the lie of being okay with casual sex, because love wasn't what I needed. It was a cover to prevent from expressing how I truly felt.

All of the rejections that happened to me caused a huge wound in my heart. That lie was the small bandage I was trying to cover it with. The more I told myself that lie, the more hurt I became. I didn't want just sex. I wanted love and I wanted to be in a committed relationship. Not only to make me feel whole, because as someone who was struggling with relationship addiction, it was also something I needed to feel alive. It was something I needed to feel better about myself as a woman. Having a man truly love me meant that I was beautiful, likable, lovable, adored, needed, worthy, and most importantly...accepted.

It took many rejections for me to realize that it wasn't because I wasn't pretty enough, popular enough, or not worthy. My beauty and my love is one of a kind, and I understand now that some men can possibly be intimidated by both, so they'll back away. As I've mentioned earlier, I have to find a man who love just like I do and appreciates what I have to offer. I understand now that I don't need to look to a man or anyone else to make me feel special or loved, because I already am.

Most importantly if I want acceptance, I have to accept myself for who I am and with what I have. In learning this new concept to appreciating self, I have stopped comparing myself to other women. That was an ongoing cycle with each man I've dating after discovering they were seeing someone else. I no longer do it,

253 | P a g e

because I believe being different or wanting to express individuality should be celebrated.

If everyone was the same in this world, the world would be boring. I'm me and I'm going to be me until I'm no longer here, so while I'm enjoying time above the ground, I have to be the best Lakia that I can be and being happy with Lakia is a must. If I'm not going to be happy about who I am then no one else will, either. It's taken many years to realize that, but the most important thing is I finally get it.

Today, you are looking at a much more confident woman with so much to offer, especially more than her vagina. I embrace life for what it is, and enjoying the beauty of it all while embracing the struggles. Embracing the struggles has helped me gain the self-acceptance that I needed in order to accept what I truly deserve from others, particularly men.

The tears that form and fall from my cheeks as I write this chapter, is followed by a smile that represents my accomplishment. I've gained self-respect as a woman when I stopped accepting bullshit. I've taken responsibility for my own happiness, and I've accepted my own unique beauty. Those other women they've stopped seeing me for were pretty, but so am I.

No man and no other woman can make me think differently about how I look. My unique inner and out beauty is enough for me. My whole being is enough PERIOD. I accept me with all my flaws. I don't compare myself to anyone anymore, and that's from a personal standpoint and a professional one. I'm blessed and highly favored. I am ready to explore love with thick skin and a healed heart and remaining optimistic about my future.

It all starts with me and my ability to foresee greatness in all aspects of my life, including love. I know that I have what it takes to build a solid loving relationship from the ground up with a man who'll truly love me. Until then, I'm appreciating the time being single and working on my personal growth. Nothing feels greater than personal growth. Part of my growth is knowing that comparisons only matter when you compare yourself today from the person you were yesterday.

Chapter 30

"Being a parent means putting your child's best interests above your own, and that means finding a way to form an amicable relationship with your ex as co-parents"~Dr. Phil

E arlier, I've mentioned that I lost two houses. One I shared with my cousin, and my own house. My current situation is not something I'm too happy about, but I had to put my pride to the side and do what was necessary for my children. After being forced out of my house, I had nowhere else to go, and I didn't want to stay in a shelter.

After much consideration, I decided to take up residency at my children's father's house. I know you're wondering why because of what I shared earlier. However, I am blessed to co-parent with a man who genuinely cares enough not to see me and his kids on the street. Even if he's just tolerating me because of the kids, I'm thankful for that, as well. I'm not saying it's the easiest to live with an ex, but I have to keep reminding myself that this is a temporary situation, until I get back on my feet as a homeowner.

This living situation has put a damper on my dating life. Where I'm staying is the primary reason of why I'm not dating. The other reason is to keep the peace in the house. After all these years, I can't help but feel like my children's father could get jealous, pick arguments, or worse put me out. If I wanted to casually date right now, it would be very frustrating. However, I feel like God has put me here for many reasons and I trust the process. As of recent months, my hours on the job have decreased drastically.

My belief is if I didn't lose my house then, I would have eventually because of the decreasing hours. Decreased hours equal a small paycheck. A small paycheck equals a distressed single mother trying to keep a roof over her children's heads. A lot of financial pressure has been near non-existent now that I'm staying in a house fully paid for and there aren't a lot of bills for me to handle.

My current living situation has given me a little financial freedom, as well as the ability to travel when necessary for my literary career. This makes it a win/lose situation for me. I'm not able to date which I shouldn't anyway in order to focus on writing, but I'm capable of saving money, and putting it towards clearing my debt, a new home, and my publishing career.

The communication him and I have depends on the day, his mood, my mood, but overall we're cordial. We both try to do things to make living together a little easier and peaceful. If I utilize his van, I'll bring it home with gas. If I need a ride to work or need to be picked up, he'll do it. He'll cook for the kids, since I come home from work late often.

It helps to remain peaceful, even with our history. I am re-instilling the respect for him as Robert's father, as well. I have to remind myself daily that everything I felt from Robert's death, he felt too. It's that unbreakable bond we'll have that I believe will keep our co-parenting amicable. That allows our son and daughter to see and feel peace between their parents. After our relationship ended in 2009, I was never the type to use my children as pawn to manipulate, hurt their dad, or force my kids to "choose sides".

It's an immature move for mothers to make when we all know children need their fathers in their lives. Why make it harder than it already is because you feel some kind of way? My Libra senses wouldn't allow me to do that. Even after my "pissed off" period with him I still found diplomatic ways to deal with him, because he has and always will be there for his children. Besides, I know what it's like to grow up without a father. Mine passed when I was six or seven years old. I have to resort to remembering bits and pieces of memories of my dad because of a freak boating accident.

My children has a dad who even though is struggling health wise, is still here to share life with them. What kind of mother would I be to hinder that? As far as dating, I won't say it's frustrating, but it can be discouraging to meet a guy I'm interested in and yet can't give any play because of where I live. The best way that I deal with this situation is to again...practice patience.

As a self-proclaimed initiator, practicing patience is idealistic for me for two reasons. The first reason is to see if the guy I'm interested in is interested enough in me to approach me. The second reason is it's a good way for me to test my will power. The time given to endure both also helps me deal with the fact that my priorities are exactly where they should be right now my writing career.

When or if I meet someone who approaches me respectfully and appears to be interested in me, I will be honest with him about my living situation. If he so chooses to fall back, I'll respect that and move on. If he's okay with it great! Either way, I'm remembering that with patience, comes the ability to accept what is and work on what I foresee.

Everything I'm experiencing now including my inability to date pushes me further in the right direction in life. Every detail in my life is responsible for the path that I'm taking. I'm working on being more responsible, more accepting, and more obedient to my own needs.

Until I walk into a room where there are a ton of men and all of their ultra fineness caressing the room, I will not yet see how strong I am from refraining from approaching a man. I know my vagina will do a couple of flips, but I won't judge my vagina and neither should you. Until then, I assume I won't allow myself to endure that kind of pressure. While my living situation gives me limitations, it also helps me fulfill a lot of what I need to do. Proper co-parenting is at the top of the list.

My children's father can be what the kids say today "irky", but I give my hats off to him for putting up with me. That's proof he loves his children, which is something I've never doubted. I'm glad their relationship is solid.

Chapter 31

"Sexuality is one of the ways that we become enlightened, actually, because it leads us to self-knowledge."~Alice Walker

A s a sexual person, practicing celibacy is very challenging, to say the least. However, it's a critical and necessary move for me to make in order to connect better with men and learn to express sexual freedom without the pressures of commitment. Love and commitment has to happen naturally and as I practice abstaining I come to discover that just like any other addiction, going through a period of withdrawal takes place.

Going through withdrawal from relationship addiction gives me that inevitable feeling of weakness that I battle with daily. I try not to let my withdrawal get the best of me by taking my mind off of sex. That includes doing any physical activity with my children, hanging out with girlfriends, or diving into my writing and publishing business head on. When I simply cannot control the urges, I get my bag. You ladies know what I mean when I say "the bag".

Waiting to have sex is easier said than done, but I'm working through it. Upon waiting, I've also come to discover a sense of empowerment that I now carry. I'm not letting my vagina take over my thoughts, or even penis for that matter. I'm taking charge on when I want to share my body, and who I share it with. Not that I haven't before, but this time it's without the confines of pressure, ultimatums, and fear of being alone. The inner conflicts that I battled with caused me to mistreat my body.

The physical aspect of sex felt great with the men I've dated, but their energy was depleting mine, as well as my spirit, my pride, and my sense of self. I became emotionally exhausted to the point of numbness. When I took on this personal challenge, I slowly began to regain a lot of my strength, and I gained more control of my mind and body. Celibacy is said to improve mental powers and concentration.

While I'm currently not getting any, my focus has gotten as thick as a football's player neck. I have spent time developing and perfecting my craft as a publisher, and just doing non-stop writing. I believe that not rushing sex makes a fresh relationship stay fresh. While the woman gently rejects the man, he in turn respects her more. I think that actually impresses the man more than what she does sexually.

I see things a lot more clearly since starting my celibacy. As I'm nearing my withdrawal period, I've come to an understanding that men want the same thing that women want and that's love. I used to wonder how men can have sex with women without strings attached. I've discovered the answer that has been my understanding. Men know what kind of woman they want, and having sex with no strings attached makes it easier for them to give and receive intimacy without guilt or emotions. They have needs just like women do, so turning down vagina is something I believe they rarely do. However, they save the emotions for the one who they'll want longevity with. You know, the one they can see themselves saying "I love you" to.

If they don't see that with you, then sex will be the only thing he'll commit with you, until he finds someone worthy of dumping you for. It's harsh, but it's the truth. I may be using my own experiences as a general theory. Nevertheless, I believe it's important for both men and women to do what's necessary to prevent confusion, drama, and heartbreak. Men struggle with the aforementioned, as well. They just deal with it differently than we do.

Chapter 32

"Forty is the old age of youth; Fifty is the youth of old age"~ Victor Hugo

I don't know if any other woman is as excited as I am to turn forty. I have another year before my fortieth birthday, and for the last ten years I said when I turn forty I will be settled and have accomplished everything I want to accomplish. It's sort of like an ultimatum that I've given to myself, and it helps push me to become my greater self. I have developed the belief that after the age of thirty-five we began to make better choices that will improve the quality of our lives.

We're no longer surrounded by drama, because we've evolved enough not to put up with it or the folks who brings us to it. By the time we turn forty, we should have shed those who brings us down and surround ourselves with positive people. By the time we hit forty, our dreams, goals, and desires should have already manifested from our hard work. When you reach the age of forty, you'll know what you want in a lover and what kind of relationship you want. Your sex life improves, as a result.

Forty is the new twenty, but a lot wiser! After a couple of decades of risk taking and poor choices, we should finally learn to look after ourselves with better decisions. Turning forty will be such a relief for me. God willing, if I make it to that age, I can look back at the emotional marathon that I ran and the career goals that seemed impossible to meet but finally happened and rejoice because I made it. Some folks are afraid of getting older, because each time you age it's a step closer to death. The truth is we're all going to die someday, but instead of focusing on death just enjoy living.

That's what I plan to do for the rest of my life. They say the age of fifty is generally the golden age but forty is the golden age for me.

Oddly enough, I see myself laid up on a beach with my umbrella drink, toasting with my loved ones on the greatness that my life have served me since turning forty. I foresee a more peaceful and stable journey in my near future.

While I currently get back on track with just about everything, I can say that I'm doing it with optimism. I have implemented personal guidelines from this point on to prevent from making repetitive actions which could hinder my growth. When I turn forty, I want to be able to say and show what "forty" is supposed to look like. Forty is supposed to look like confidence, stability, self-love, and a go-getter, all wrapped up in a glittery package labeled "priceless".

Besides bad decision making, there are a few other things I can happily stop doing and won't be ashamed about. As I've gotten older, I realize that staying up on fads and trends in music and fashion is something that I don't need to do. After the age of twenty-five, we should really stop trying to "fit in". I'm feeling freedom in knowing that I don't have to be in the know with every fad or trend. I don't have to prove that I'm beautiful to anyone. You can see beauty in my eyes and in my smile. I smile because I overcame many obstacles in my life from petty mistakes to extreme tragedy.

To this day, I'm heading towards complete acceptance of everything, and that's what keeps me smiling. It's also what keeps my eyes bright by looking ahead and never looking back. As I approach forty, I feel more comfortable in my own skin, calmer about the challenges I face, and I'm able to function better in all my relationships. I also look a hell of a lot better, because I have more money than I did when I was in my twenties. When you have a bank account with actual money in it, it changes things. Responsibility is sexy. Responsibility at forty is even sexier.

Chapter 33

"Whatever you want in life, other people are going to want it too. Believe in yourself enough to accept the idea that you have an equal right to do it."~ Diane Sawyer

I t's taken me years to fully believe in accomplishing my dream. Even after the release of my first book, I still had doubts that I could become successful. Of course, that may have to do with my lack of work ethic as an author, but I think part of the reason why I didn't put forth effort is because I didn't believe that I could have the kind of success that would land me on national television.

I've heard from many independent authors in the literary game share their story of how major book retailers are really fickle when it comes to indie authors or authors who aren't well-known. Some have even stopped writing, as a result. However, I still believed that I had a chance, until I saw lackluster sales. My book wasn't getting enough buzz out of my hometown, so I became highly discouraged. The industry itself became discouraging with the decline of paperbacks, "cliques" within the industry who only supported who they personally know, and the closing of a lot of African- American owned book stores.

It was all enough to make me quit the business altogether, but my passion for writing wouldn't allow me to do it. Even when I felt that my second book would not become a blockbuster, I still wrote it and published it. I released it with a less than enthusiastic attitude. Again, that resulted in me not promoting well, and basically not giving a damn if it flopped. I wrote two books and that's all that mattered.

After a while I felt undeserving of feeling the accomplishment of anything, because of what was going on in the business, and not giving my all. I felt like there was no room for me at the top in the African-American literary industry. It wasn't until I felt the need to succeed in something when I decided to shift my focus and dedication into a better direction. I needed to feel like a more confident woman, and what better way to do that than to accomplish something you love to do?

I've realized I took advantage of the gift God gave me and became lazy. I became highly disappointed in myself for not trying harder, and letting others influence my decision. Deep down inside, I know I have what it takes to become a successful author. I just need to work harder as if my life depends on it.

No other publisher said it would be easy publishing a book, so I was not surprised about the hard work and money I had to put up to publish one. I was discouraged, lazy, and again looking for success to knock on my door. I took a long hard look at myself and realized that I wanted a different kind of success for all of the wrong reasons.

I understand now that if we're going into this business with fame and money on the brain, then we won't make it. I was also competitive with myself, having to prove to myself that I could do better than before. Other authors on the grind were getting more buzz, some were first time authors. Other folks I know personally were on the come up with their talents and passion. I couldn't help but become a little green with envy, but that only pushed me further to become greater.

Remember the epiphany I mentioned having in an earlier chapter? That's when I got my shit together. It was right around the time when I had enough of limiting myself, and needing something to live and breathe for. I eat, sleep, breathe, and live writing, so why wasn't I producing in my passion. The enthused attitude I had when I finished typing my first book's manuscript was nowhere to be found. I wanted that enthusiasm and confidence back. It seemed like everyone around me was succeeding in whatever they were doing but me. I understand that it was their time to shine, so I needed to work hard enough for my star to shine, as well.

Diane Sawyer's quote is a reminder that I have every right to want success and reach for it like everyone else, but I have to genuinely want it with more idealistic inspirations, not just for fame and money. I also had to believe in myself more, because no one else will if I don't. As I continue to perfect my craft as a writer and publisher, I feel that familiar sense of enthusiasm that I've lost in the beginning of my career. I find it necessary to continue to compete with myself. I must do better than I have before.

My belief is that the outcome from competing with myself will result in more opportunities for me. I deserve a chance at success, as I had when I initially began my career, but I understand that it takes time to build success. With time, comes hard work which will eventually pay off.

Like I said before I'm no quitter, and whatever stumbling block I come across I'll make my way around with persistence. I don't know what's ahead as I approach the height of my literary career. I may actually become rich and famous or I may flop, but one thing's for sure... no one can ever say I didn't try. Even if I flop I will continue to write, because it's what I eat, breathe, and live.

I have more than enough faith and believe that all it takes is one step to make a difference. If we believe in us enough to make that move, then we will come across good things. I'm no longer lazy, and I plan to be the best I can be in this business. I would be lying if I said fame and money is no longer on the brain. However, it's not the primary focus of my ambition.

I want to be known as a great writer and as a publisher who helps make to make that aspiring author's dream come true. I'm in this business to stay, and I refuse to let anything or anyone discourage me this time around. God blesses all of us at different times in our lives.

While some have completed their journeys and succeeded, I take into consideration that others are still traveling through theirs. I am one of those people still traveling through her journey. Fortunately, there are fewer stumbling blocks which mean I'm nearing completion. I believe in myself to complete the journey and celebrate not giving up. I owe it to my readers, my children, and myself.

Chapter 34

"I did then what I knew how to do. Now that I know better, I do better."~Maya Angelou

It's odd to look back at all the bad decisions I've made and realizing that I could have made better choices. It takes great courage to acknowledge that I didn't because I was "comfortable" with the choices I made. I thought the choices I made WERE the better choices for me at the time. Now that I know better, I do better. I still make bad decisions today, but I accept them with hopes in learning from them and doing my best not to repeat them. I understand that making bad choices is a part of life. They are responsible in some way to help you evolve. I'm living my life the way I'm supposed to from the bad choices I've made throughout my life.

Looking back, even up to my most recent personal challenge, I realized I had a lot of growing up to do spiritually and emotionally. I had to check myself on blaming others for whatever was going wrong in my life when in fact, I was the one to blame. God somehow takes us through trials to see how much wiser we become out of them, or fearless, happier, or even how much we've had enough of the repetitive outcomes of our choices.

Sometimes, I wonder if some of us use other's accomplishments in their relationships and careers as motivation. I know I have, and that became a disaster. I let the accomplishments of others intimidate me, and when I thought the outcome would be similar, I felt like I took my biggest fall when it didn't. However, I learned from doing so that I have to follow my own road to success and better relationships.

What works for others may not work for me. I'm sure we all have looked back and seen situations where we wished we had handled things differently. For me, I have to remember not to beat myself up about it, because I acted with the level of knowledge and capabilities that I had at the time. Now, I have a better understanding of how to handle myself in a similar situation that I know I'll have to challenge again in the future. Because of what I've learned, I have a higher state of awareness than I had back then. I look at my past experiences as platforms and motivation for continued growth.

Some of the outcomes of my choices are still affecting me today, but I know that they won't limit me in any way, shape, or form unless I allow them. I'm doing better with accepting my past so that I can deal accordingly with my present. That way, I can control how my future should be.

As long as we have the belief that there are infinite possibilities for us to achieve greatness in all aspects of our lives, every negative situation we've had will NOT have the power to hold us back. I'm becoming the story that people can read and use to become better. My past negative experiences are there for me to stay humble, yet proud for overcoming. My past negative experiences are also there to prove to others that they are not alone in their journeys to improve. However, I'm always learning and evolving, so I'm not going to settle for who I am right now.

I like where I am emotionally, spiritually, and even financially but I can always improve. I'm at peace with my current life so much so that

I anticipate what's next with an open mind, open arms, and a better attitude. I'm internally celebrating and it reflects in the smile that I carry.

Chapter 35

"The law is simply this: We attract whatever we think about, good or bad."~ From the book " The Laws of Attraction".

I use the Laws of Attraction to help simplify and beautify my life. It starts with my thought process, and how I let them consume me. Back when I use to allow negative thoughts to enter my mind, it affected me to the point where I started worrying about situations that weren't even in existence. The Laws of Attraction have taught me about shifting my thought process in a more positive direction. Positive thinking makes the universe aware of what you desire in life. We attract both good and bad experiences based on our thoughts. If we think we're broke, we will be. If we think we're lonely, we will feel it. If you think with a cluttered mind, you will not function well in life. I think you get the picture.

When I decided to focus more on my publishing and writing career, my thoughts were that it would become solidified as a legit business. Since then, I did the necessary paperwork to make it official with an LLC. It's proof that dreams and goals become a reality when we focus more on it. Because I dream about making it daily and my focus has been on ten, I'm creating my reality by attracting the experiences that I need.

This in turn lets the universe bring me what I'm working hard for. My intuition has been my life's guide for better decision making these days. I listen to it, instead of over-thinking and over-analyzing situations. It's beneficial for me to trust my intuition. It's like an alarm that goes off when I feel something isn't right. If my Libra scales feel unbalanced, I make a conscious choice to remove the dead weight of a situation that I don't need in my life. I know it's something that is preventing me from moving forward.

As a result, I listen carefully to my intuition and allow it to guide my emotions and my thinking. This helps maintain a more peaceful life that I deserve to live. The universe gives me the internal power to do this. Another law of attraction says that in order to make change, we have to vision things differently than how they are now. I go to bed every night, foreseeing a better writing career. If I see it, then I can achieve it. Along the way, I avoid negative thinking, as well as doubtful people. I don't allow self-doubt to creep up, because that is the death of all possibilities.

By living a life full of positivity, including my thinking I am attracting abundance in all aspects of my life. I deserve happiness and success just like everyone else. If I can use my magnetic inner power to enhance my chances that only means that the universe is sending me everything that I deserve.

The universe sees that I make it my daily mission to block all forms of negativity. It sees that I'm getting out of my own way and ridding the fear I use to carry. It sees that I'm no longer limiting myself. Even when I become disappointed about anything, I don't stay submerged in the feeling of disappointment, because I focus on how to become not as disappointed the next time.

If it's something I want, I'll work hard to get it. If it's something I don't want, I'll get rid of it. It's that simple. Again, my Libra scales need to stay balanced. The laws of attraction are the ultimate source to a more satisfying life for anyone. I suggest everyone who needs uplifting to follow them, because they have helped me tremendously.

Chapter 36

"A change in bad habits leads to a change in

life."~ Jenny Craig

My mistakes often came with repetition. From something as small as bad eating to a more serious habit like loveless sex, they were my habits that I clearly needed to break. There are a few bad habits that I still struggle with today, but thankfully the ones I were strong enough to break helped me design life-changing and necessary moves. We break our habits when we get tired of seeing no change or the same results, which can be very discouraging.

It has taken me a long time to understand that my lifestyle was triggering my habit-forming ways. For example, because of my relationship addiction, my habit was having meaningless sex. As an emotional eater, my addiction to junk food became my source to feel better, even if it was temporary. My bad habits kept me in one place where I felt stuck like sand buried at my ankles. I had to change my behavior for me to break my habit, but I didn't know how at the time. I wasn't yet aware of the power that has always existed in me to want to change.

The power to accept and love myself was the filter that changed my ways. When I changed how I looked at myself, I stopped doing things that made me feel stuck in one place. I was able to strengthen the new behavior that I now carry and suppress the original with optimism. My new behavior came with self-awareness and with more confidence.

Wanting to reach goals and having a better life was pretty much on my "to-do" list, as you obviously can tell. I would be still struggling had I not become aware of my bad habits and dealing with them accordingly. Most I've gotten rid of, but some I still struggle with. I'm human and as I say continuously throughout this book, I'm a work in progress.

I'm aware that I need to break every one of them if I want a more productive life. Loveless sex and eating bad were not my only bad habits. Here are some others and how I've dealt or currently deal with each one.

- **Thinking negatively**

  This was primarily my reason for failing in a lot of my personal challenges. From fear of failure to blaming others for my problems, negative thinking caused me to make self-sabotaging decisions. That is, until I discovered the power in me to change my way of thinking and also following The Laws of Attraction.

- **Gossiping**

   I must admit, I gossip every now and then.
   With the popularity of reality shows, the
   internet where information about public
   figures is highly accessible, and
   unavoidable current events, it's hard not
   to talk about something or someone.
   However, I don't make it my daily mission
   to blow up someone's phone to discuss
   who Jason screwed and what Lisa wore to
   the club the other day. That's not my
   style.

- **Seeking attention**

   I'm extra guilty of this habit, because I
   needed attention from men who wasn't
   giving me any. Ranting on social media,
   hoping he'll respond was my way of

seeking attention. I checked myself when I realized he didn't pay me any mind with the "no answer" response. I needed attention so bad that I was prepared to have confrontational conversations with these men, and with no care about how I looked online.

- **Resisting change**

This was a habit that kept me from evolving. I was afraid of change because I was comfortable with settling. It wasn't until I realized I still wasn't fully happy that I stopped being intimated with my own potential, and got out of my own way.

- **Making rash decisions**

Oddly, making rash decisions wasn't much of a habit unless it involved a man and being DICKmatized. I simply broke this habit when I decided to care for my vagina better.

- **Being defensive**

  It's a habit that I still struggle with to this day. I mentioned earlier that I sometimes confuse constructive criticism with not so constructive criticism. I get defensive either way. I have to be mindful that others only critique what they are familiar with. It's my job to explain what they're not familiar with in hopes they'll get a better understanding.

- **Procrastinating**

It's another habit that I still struggle with to this day. Hence, this book that I've taken two years to finish.

- **Multitasking**

- This is a habit that I used to think wouldn't affect me, until I realize one day that my brain cannot catch up fast enough with my body. Doing numerous projects at once is a stressful task, and I respect anyone who can do it with no problem.

- **Engaging in self-sabotage**

  Again, something else I struggle with today and working to improve. Emotional eating has been a habit for quite some time. The older I become, the more apparent the effects are from years of bad eating. I deal with it by with exercising, eating less McDonalds, and eating more fruits and veggies, and drinking tons of water.

- **Being a maladaptive perfectionist**

  This habit was my cause for much self-criticism. When my quest to become "perfect" in anything didn't happen, I became very critical of myself to the point where I became depressed. I felt better about my screw ups when I accepted that perfection is the ultimate illusion of life. I'm okay with being perfectly imperfect.

When we break a habit, it can give you a rewarding feeling. Breaking habits means that we've accomplished getting rid something that could be detrimental to your personal evolution. Although I still struggle with a few, I am aware that I can still conquer them. It takes time. With time, comes patience. I'm patient with myself, and I'm aware of my capabilities. We'll do what we need to do when we're ready to see change in our lives. I want to see complete change from my inside to my outside. I speak full change into existence. I can and will break all of my bad habits. My bad habits will not break me.

Chapter 37

"Life's journey is always easier when you hear a

friend's footsteps beside you"!

Unknown

W hile going through my journey

towards success, I've realized that

taking my journey comes with sacrifice. My

sacrifice is not feeling that close bond with my

friends like I used to feel. Before I left my role as

co-host with the radio show gig, I was always out

and about with my girls, bonding, connecting,

and feeling like nothing will change that, even

when we were a part. Most of the time, we attended events not only as what we were collectively to the public, but as girlfriends hanging out.

Now that I'm taking a personal journey outside of the group, I can't help but feel that my leaving has changed the dynamic of my friendship with them. We don't talk as much as we used to and it bothers me. However, I understand that this is what I basically asked for. I became spoiled with their attention and time, and I wanted them to "hold my hand" while going on this journey with me. When I say "hold my hand", I wanted the support that I was looking for as if I was still a part of the group. I didn't yet comprehend the fact that when I left the group, I severed the maximum support system, too.

I've accepted that they're not obligated to do certain things for me because we're friends. They have their own business to promote, so I have to respect that. I'm also accepting the fact that this is not their journey to take.

As a friend, I have to understand that stepping away also means that they have to go through the rest of their journey with the changes that I've forced upon them. I'm learning to accept that even friends will have to separate at some point in their lives by taking different directions throughout their journeys.

The cost of ambition and taking that personal journey to our own success will force us to do many things alone, and I'm becoming okay with that. It's necessary because we need to stay focused and dedicated. Otherwise, our journey will turn into a never-ending quest.

I want to assume that my friends are just giving me the time and space that I need while I go through my journey. Not having that girlfriend bond that I used to have with them is the toughest part about it, but I have to understand that if my social life with them was still in full effect today, I'd never get anything done. I'm taking this as a sign that my extra free time is exactly what I need to prioritize and focus.

Acceptance and embracing change is a part of my journey. I continue to think positively about it all and I shift my needs from needing my hand held to owning the fact that I heavily fucks with myself. I know my girls support me, but this journey isn't about them. This journey isn't just about becoming successful in business but personally, as well. It's about re-discovering who I am, progressing at my own pace, and being at peace with being alone while I do it all. Most importantly, I'm learning that true friendship isn't defined by how much support I receive.

Honestly, support comes in many different forms. My inner voice tells me the support from my girls was apparent the moment they told me goodbye and allowed me to spread my wings without anger or judgment. When I reach the end of my journey, I know they'll be there waiting with open arms. Nevertheless, I'm enjoying the personal journey that I'm taking. I'm discovering a lot about myself along the way.

Although I miss my girls, I'm appreciating the time to myself, as I continue to figure out who I am as Lakia. I know what I want for the brand Lakia Nichole, thanks to what I'm learning and discovering on my journey. Figuring who Lakia really is outside of the brand is not too far behind. I'm getting there. I'm a work in progress.

Chapter 38

"Trust is built with consistency"~ Lincoln Chafee

C onsistency is one of many traits I look for in a man I take interest in. Actually, consistency is usually at the top of the list along with good sex. When I discovered what I was missing in relationships with men, the conclusion came to me in a conversation with God. A lot of what I was not getting from a man was some things that I wasn't giving myself, and consistency was one of them. How could I want a man who practices consistency when I'm not consistent with my own damn self? It's funny how things finally make sense when we find out it doesn't make sense.

I was inconsistent with being consistent, and it reflected in my failed business plans and in my love life. I shifted gears when I decided to do the requirements that I needed from others. I now practice consistency without stopping short of maximum satisfaction. In turn, I have become more productive with my business needs and everything else in my life that is meaningful to me.

I use to think being consistent was for perfectionists, but that couldn't be farther from the truth. It's a matter of making progress, and achieving some level of success in most areas of life. This is the type of action that I don't mind repeating. Practicing consistency is essential for a more prosperous life.

From trying to lose weight to staying on top of the literary game, consistency gives me that push inch by inch to being the best version of myself in all areas of my life. I'm also learning to not be too hard on myself when things don't go as planned. Again, my goal is not to become perfect.

Consistency is not an essential action for perfection. It's an essential action for progression. I think the key to maintaining consistency is planning for failure. This may sound odd, but think about it. Lots a people fail at remaining consistent with their goals or breaking habits, because they don't have a plan for dealing with failure. As I work on maintaining consistency, I'm learning to be prepared for anything that could go wrong while going through my journey. Planning on how to deal with failure can help us get back on track to consistency. This includes love and relationships.

Speaking from experience, lack of consistency can ruin a relationship. It's my belief that when we maintain consistency in a relationship, it could help solidify the foundation to a great relationship. Think about it! When we meet someone and decide we like that person, we are attracted to the person based on their characteristic traits when we meet.

Personally, a man doing what he says he's going to do and remains consistent with his word is a plus in my book, especially after such an intimate act like sexual intercourse. It provides a certain kind of confidence with knowing he's genuinely into me, and that's very important to me, because I have yet to experience that.

Overall, consistency becomes a pattern in which you develop in order to receive and maintain progression. From a business standpoint, consistency creates the reputation that your business will be built on. From a relationship standpoint, consistency will build the foundation you need. From a personal standpoint, consistency will help you progress in whatever you desire to achieve. Now that I practice consistency, I don't feel as bad wanting it from others, particularly men.

Chapter 39

"When you lose something, it just means that you

deserve better. Be patient."~Unknown

I t has taken a long time for me to accept that I deserve better than what I allowed in relationships with men. Part of my acceptance was learning that everything I deserve starts with me and no one else. Now that I go above and beyond to not mistreat myself, I refuse to be mistreated by anyone else. My dedication to loving myself fully has reinforced the confidence that I need, and not accepting anything less than what I deserve from a man. As the Maya Angelou quote is read, "when you know better, you do better."

I knew better when I wanted more in relationships, but didn't know how to get it. I did better when I decided to give it to myself the way I wanted it. I gave myself an abundance of self-love, which in turn advanced to self-respect. Part of my personal journey to personal evolution is finding out who I am.

I've discovered that I am a woman of substance who has had enough of mediocrity in her life. I'm striving for love and respect by dedicating to showing myself those needs. I strive to be an influence to those I connect with to show me love and respect, as well. When others see how you treat yourself, you set the bar to a level of how they should treat you.

During my journey, I've come to discover the two things that we usually take for granted have played a major part in my personal transformation and that's time and patience. Time and patience has helped me to see what I've done wrong. Time has given me the recognition within myself to become greater and receive what I'm worthy of. Patience has helped me work through my emotional challenges thoroughly without worry or frustration. I'm accepting the fact that I cannot change the past.

The best reward will be showing those that I've allowed to mistreat me that I never needed their love and attention to begin with. I understand now that the love and attention I needed was my responsibility to give. I'm showing those that I should have been respected then, just as much as I showed them respect. I must say that in order to become at peace about my past, I have to forgive in order to move on. Not only forgive the guys I dated for mistreating me, but I had to forgive myself for allowing the mistreatment.

My lack of knowledge in knowing how to provide emotionally for myself was the main cause of my many disappointments with men. I didn't know that at the time. I looked to men to make me happier.

Today, as I continue to strive for progress in all areas in my life, I am reminded of how emotionally and spiritually confused I was in the past. Since my transformation, communication with others is easier. My journey has taught me to be more expressive without fear of criticism. My relationships with everyone from family to friends have become a little more solid, and I walk with the confidence in knowing that I overcame adversity.

As I've mentioned earlier, I am a woman of substance and nothing and no one can change that. My son and daughter will read my story one day, and will become proud of their mother's accomplishments. They will know what it takes to not quit in life, because I'm living proof.

Earlier, I've mentioned about using my experiences to figure out what I am.

All of what I've shared in this book has taught me two main things that I'm certain of. My adversities didn't break me, I broke my adversities. Therefore, my journey has taught me

that I'm... unbroken.

The End